SKIRTS:

Sew Your Own!

SKIRTS

Sew Your Own!

GISELLA HEINEMANN

Illustrated by the Author

McGRAW-HILL BOOK COMPANY

New York   St. Louis   San Francisco   Bogotá   Düsseldorf   Madrid   Mexico
          Montreal   Panama   Paris   São Paulo   Tokyo   Toronto

First edition, 1978

1234567890 HAHA 78321098

Library of Congress Cataloging in Publication Data

Heinemann, Gisella.
  Skirts.

    1. Skirts.   I. Title.
TT540.H44   646.4′3   78-1342
ISBN 0-07-027940-3

To my mother, Erna Gross

CONTENTS

INTRODUCTION

I have been a designer of skirts and other sportswear for many years. At one time I owned a factory that manufactured my clothes for boutiques and department stores throughout the country.

Since a number of women in the publishing industry have worn my skirts and have been enthusiastic about them, it was inevitable, I suppose, that someone would approach me to write a book about skirtmaking. In addition to my years of experience in designing and sewing, I had just spent a year and a half writing a novel. It would make sense to combine both skills to produce a book on skirtmaking for the home sewer. But I hesitated when asked to write the book, because I believe most how-to books cheat people. Directions are too often incomplete, illustrations too often confusing. One never actually learns to do whatever it is the book sets out to teach. Only if I could think of a way to give real information would I undertake the project, I decided.

As I thought about how to do a truly useful book on sewing, I came up with the idea of including actual foldout patterns in the book. To my knowledge, this had never been done before. Using only one-size-fits-everyone styles in the book would be a logical way to carry out that idea. Numerous, accurate, step-by-step instructional drawings would be essential, too. Since most sewers find zippers a chore, I chose designs that did not require them.

By keeping all these elements in mind, I think I have succeeded in writing for the home sewer a useful, honest book—one that will enrich her sewing skills and open up her creative channels as well.

There are seven basic skirt designs in this book, with dozens of variations and many suggestions for the trim or fabric or color or belt that will make your skirt unique.

All the styles (except one) have been successfully manufactured by me and have therefore been tested for fit by women throughout the country. They are, every one of them, easy to cut, easy to sew, and easy to wear. And to help you sew a little faster and more simply, I've included some of the tricks of the sewing industry. I have assumed in writing the book that the reader already knows how to sew, but even so you should read the general instructions in the first chapter carefully.

A simple skirt in a good fabric and a beautiful color does not need excessive trims. Think of a trim that is unique, one that you admire, and use it. Flip through the book for ideas before deciding on any one skirt. But I don't want you to sew just the skirts I suggest. Rather, after making a few skirts, expand on this book yourself.

I'd like to give a special thank-you to Theresa Bucchichio, who helped me immeasurably in the chapter on sewing and cutting tips. She was my sample maker in the factory, my right arm, and is now a sewing teacher for the High School of Fashion in New York City. She stresses common sense in sewing above all things. Sometimes when we'd work out a new design, she'd say, "Let me see it in my hand, under the needle. Then I'll be able to tell you the best way to make it." The implication, of course, is that the garment itself tells you how to sew it if you just apply common sense. Another lesson I learned from Theresa is that the sewer is in control, not the fabric.

I suggest to you, then, that when making up the skirts in the book, you should reread the instructions with the fabric in your hand. Often, this will make things clear to you.

As you begin to experiment with the ideas in this book, don't be afraid. There is almost nothing you can do wrong. No one notices, when the garment is on, if the seams were sewn a little crooked or if the gathers aren't that even. Of course, I'm not saying you shouldn't try for perfection. But really, who and what is perfect? Remember: *Sewing is easy. Relax and enjoy it!*

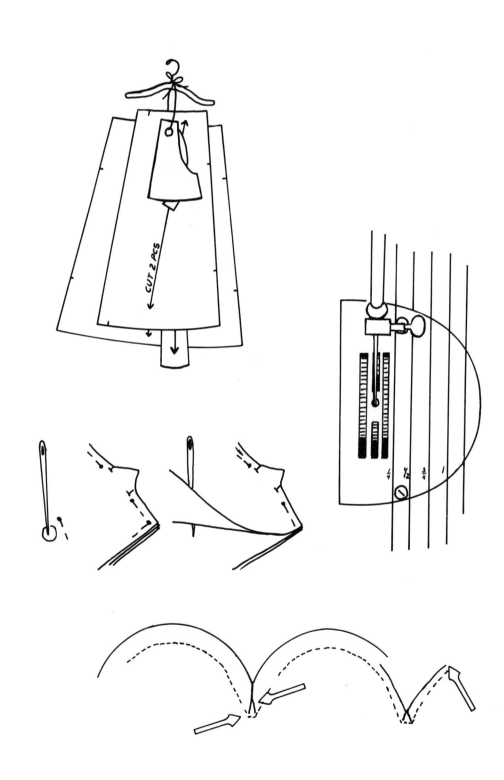

CHAPTER ONE

SOME GENERAL INSTRUCTIONS TO SIMPLIFY SEWING

CARE OF THE PATTERNS

You will find in an envelope in the back of this book patterns for four skirts. The following is a list of the pattern pieces you should have. Check to make sure you have them all. We decided, in an effort to save space, not to include the belt pattern piece. The belt is described in detail in each cutting guide, and is really very simple to cut.

If you take care of these patterns, there is no reason why you shouldn't be able to use them for the rest of your life. And this is how to take care of them: Get some large sheets of uncreased wrapping paper or construction paper—the kind children use for school projects. Most art stores have it. You can even use brown package-wrapping paper—the kind that comes in rolls. In fact, any paper can be used, as long as it is flexible and sturdy.

Fig. 1

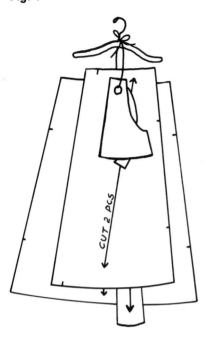

CUT 2 PCS

Next, using a tracing wheel or any method you find easier, trace each pattern onto the heavier paper. Be sure to weight down the tissue as you trace so that the pattern won't shift. Then immediately transfer all the markings and instructions to the traced pattern. Cut it out, cut a small circle or punch a hole in the center top of each piece, and tie all the pieces of each style together. Put this collection on a hanger, and hang it in your closet (Fig. 1). You now have a permanent pattern.

If a pattern piece in the group enclosed, or in a commercial one, is marked "on the fold," you should do the following when you transfer it to a permanent state: Place the edge of the pattern piece marked "on the fold" to the edge of a creased (folded) paper. Trace it and then cut it out. In that way, when you open the paper, you will have the whole pattern piece to use when making your *marker*. (See instructions for marker in Cutting Tips, pages 12 and 13.) Why a whole piece? Because using it enables you to maneuver the pattern pieces around, see the whole garment, and, in this way, save money by making a "tighter" marker and cutting a more accurate garment. The enclosed patterns marked "on the fold" were drawn this way only to save space.

A word of caution: Be sure to reproduce all the markings!

SKIRT	PATTERN PIECES	
Gore	1 pattern piece	1 piece
Shaped Wrap	1 front 1 back 1 placket 1 pocket 1 pocket facing	5 pieces
A-line Drawstring	1 front 1 back 1 facing	3 pieces
Shaped Patchwork Wrap	1 piece A 1 piece B 1 piece C 1 piece D 1 strip	5 pieces

CARE OF YOUR SEWING MACHINE

Your sewing machine needs to be oiled frequently. Be sure to unthread the machine before you start. Read your manual to check the oil points. If you have lost the manual, or never got one, some good rules to follow are these: Tilt the machine to expose the underside, and, using a small brush, clean out any lint you find there. Then oil the moving parts under the machine, return it to the upright position, and put a drop of oil into each visible hole in the head.

When you next sew, wipe the surface, the needle bar, and the presser foot. As a matter of fact, you should keep a soft cloth or tissues handy, and make it a habit to wipe the machine before you start sewing. Oil has a sneaky way of appearing long after it should. Run up a few seams on a scrap of fabric to work out any oil that may have settled in the needle.

Ideally the machine should be oiled after every eight hours of use.

*

If your machine does not have a seam guide on the throat plate, make one with nail polish. Remove the presser foot before you do the markings. With the needle in the hole, measure $\frac{1}{4}$ inch, $\frac{1}{2}$ inch, $\frac{3}{4}$ inch, 1 inch, etc., from the needle hole, and draw a line from the back of the throat plate to the front in the nail polish (Fig. 2). That way, you never have to premark, or measure seams as you sew. You just put the edge of the fabric to the width of the seam you want, and you'll sew a straight seam. There are many different kinds of throat plates, but the distance from the needle hole is always the same.

Use the right size needle for the right fabric. Logic is the guide here. Smaller needles, such as no. 11, are for silks and sheers, and larger ones are for heavier fabrics. Have a "vocabulary" of needles on hand.

Check for burrs, or rough spots on the point of the needle. The best way is to feel for them (with the machine turned off, of course!). There is no telling when burrs will appear on a needle. You'll only notice them by the enlarged holes, or runlike tears next to the stitching. So, check for them.

*

Fig. 2

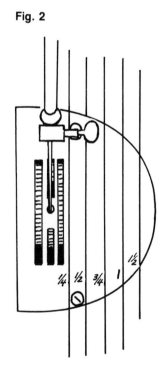

Always empty your bobbin before putting a new color on it, because there is nothing more upsetting than thinking that you have a long way to go on a bobbin, then running out in the middle of a seam. The result is sewing without thread, and having to repeat the whole step again.

Give yourself the luxury of extra bobbins, so that you can keep the half-used bobbins of black or white or navy, colors you use all the time, for quick little repair jobs.

Don't try to save money by using your grandmother's old thread. Thread weakens with age. Test it for strength. It should have some resilience. You can use cotton, or mercerized thread, by the way, for everything!

Fig. 3

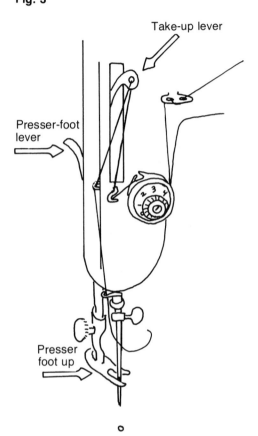

Take-up lever

Presser-foot lever

Presser foot up

USING THE MACHINE

The actual starting and ending of a seam is so important that I'd like to review it with you. If you do it correctly, you will save yourself the pain and annoyance of jammed machines, broken threads, and threads pulling out of the needle's eye.

Begin and end every seam with backtacking! If you've never heard that word or expression, it means to *reinforce* the seam.

Turn the handwheel (balance wheel) forward, *always forward*, until the take-up lever is at its highest point (Fig. 3). The needle will then be at its highest too.

Make sure the presser foot is up. Slip the fabric—its edge aligned with the correct seam allowance on the guide—under the needle. Holding the threads to the back with your left hand, turn the wheel with your right until the needle is inserted in the fabric. When starting, needle should be $\frac{1}{2}$ inch from the top edge.

Lower the presser foot to hold the fabric in place, and put the stitch lever into reverse position. Sew slowly, while still holding threads back with your left hand. When you reach the edge (Fig. 4a), put the lever into forward position and stitch (Fig. 4b). You no longer need to hold the thread, but can use *both* your hands *in front* to guide the fabric. *Never* pull the fabric from the rear as you sew!

To end a seam, stitch to the bottom edge, put machine into reverse, and sew over stitches for $\frac{1}{2}$ inch, raise lever to highest point, lift presser foot, and pull thread and fabric to rear. Clip threads. In this way, the thread will not pull out of the needle and will remain threaded for the next seam.

Fig. 4

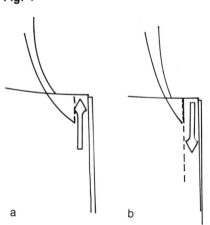

a   b

My final word about the home machine is that, with care, it will last longer than your lifetime. My mother still uses the machine she bought herself in 1920. She's made clothes with it for herself, her husband, her three daughters, and her grandchildren. She has made everything from summer playsuits to winter coats. She has made curtains, drapes, slipcovers, blankets, and quilts. And all, every one of her projects, on a small Singer portable that is about to go into its sixtieth year of use. Of course, she takes care of it!

SOME SIMPLIFIED SEWING TECHNIQUES

There is seldom any need to baste. Can you imagine the amount of time it would take if factory sewing-machine operators basted each garment? The cost to the consumer would be enormous.

Just pin. Use the right kind of pins—fairly thin ones, called "silk pins" in the stores. Any five-and-dime store carries them.

Pin as in Fig. 5. The presser foot will go right over them. Be sure the head of the pin is well out of the way of the foot and needle.

Fig. 5

*

Never pull the fabric from the rear as you stitch. The machine "feeds" the fabric without your help. Pulling makes waves and uneven tensions.

*

Fig. 6

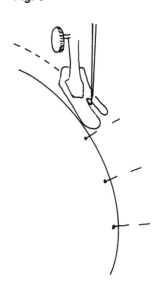

Sew at a steady slowish pace. In the long run, for the home sewer, this is the fastest, because you'll have more control over the machine and fabric. More control means fewer errors. With both hands on the fabric, in front of the needle, guide lightly. Think of your hands as part of the machine.

*

There is no reason for more than $\frac{1}{2}$-inch seam. On necks, use a $\frac{1}{4}$-inch seam, or the width of the foot, from needle to outside edge of foot (Fig. 6). Using a $\frac{1}{4}$-inch seam eliminates the need for clipping. (Armholes are the exception—they always require a $\frac{3}{8}$-inch seam.)

*

Fig. 7

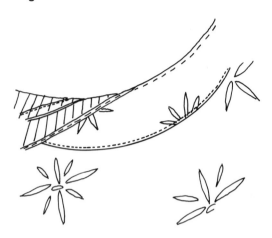

No matter how you feel about certain small sewing details, there are some you can't avoid and/or simplify. Stitching a curved facing flat is one of them.

With the right side up, and using small stitches, sew through seam on facing and body of garment close to seam line (Fig. 7).

*

The tendency on most machines is to push (feed) the upper fabric forward at a faster pace than the lower. Therefore, check notches as you sew, and, holding your hand close to the needle, ease the upper fabric under the foot while retarding the lower fabric. All this gently, gently. It takes practice, but not much, to get this habit.

Remember! *You* control both the machine and the fabric! In factories, operators almost never pin. They sew guided only by the notches. The trick, they tell me, is in their hands.

*

For gathers, use the biggest stitch your machine has. Two rows are better than one, really. Three, superb. The fabric "lays" flatter, and is more even in the sewing when there is more than one row (Fig. 8).

Leave long threads, about 6 inches, at either end of stitching line. At one end, wrap the threads around a straight pin (Fig. 9), and pull and ease from the other. The bottom (bobbin) thread pulls easier than the top.

Fig. 8

Fig. 9

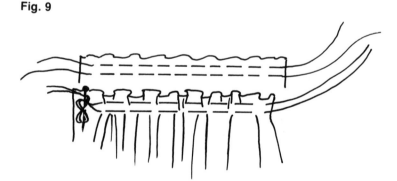

Fig. 10

If you are gathering a very long piece, such as a ruffle, do it in sections (Fig. 10). In that way, if you have bad luck, and the thread breaks, you don't have the whole thing to do over, but just the section that broke.

*

Always sew in the same direction. If you are making a skirt, sew from the waist down to the hem on both sides. Since there is, as I mentioned previously, a slight shift in the fabric, sewing in the same direction eliminates the opposition of shifts—making waves.

*

Try very hard to have center seams meet and to have notches meet. If necessary to insure this, pin at these points.

But, don't drive yourself crazy if these matches are "off" a small amount—a small amount is $\frac{1}{8}$ to $\frac{1}{4}$ inch. When my mother first taught me to sew, I would rip and rerip until I had everything perfect. There is no reason for that. It is almost impossible to detect a slightly "off" seam. Just consider the size of your body, in relation to an eighth or so of an inch. For that matter, if your seams aren't exactly straight, so what?

The exception to this rule, is, of course, a complicated and tightly fitted garment. However, in most sewing, and in just about all garments in this book, you can relax, try your best, and accept the results. Don't make sewing a chore.

*

Start darts at the wide end and sew toward the point. As you near the point, for greater control, make the last few stitches by turning the wheel by hand, rather than by using the power. The last two or three stitches should be exactly on the edge of the fabric (Fig. 11). With the needle at its highest point and the presser foot up, pull threads to the rear and cut them so that they are long enough to tie. Knot them and clip threads short, as in Fig. 12. I find a pin useful for this—put it in the center of the loose knot and keep it close to the fabric, then pull thread. If you have great control over your machine, you needn't do this handwork— you can simply backtack over these last few stitches.

I am a fairly skilled sewer, but on silks and sheers, I always use the knot method since it creates less bulk.

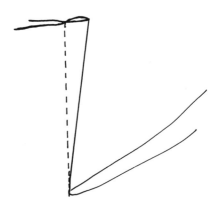

Fig. 11

Fig. 12

There is generally no reason to press seams open until the garment is completed. I can hear sewing instructors gasping with horror at that statement! But just hold seams flat with your hands when you must sew over them.

Fig. 13

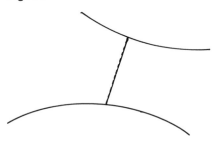

On sleeveless garments, stitch through shoulder seam line to hold facing in place (Fig. 13). Turn the wheel by hand to do this, and be sure to backtack! If done correctly, this stitching line will not show.

Velvets, velveteens, corduroys, and all other napped fabrics are cut with the nap "up." That simply means that the nap—which is the direction that is smooth to the touch and which can be determined by feeling the fabric—should go toward the waist for a skirt, and toward the neckline for a blouse or jacket. Consider the top of your body, your head, as the up side for nap.

    When cutting napped fabric, you will need more yardage, since all pieces must be aligned in the same direction (Fig. 14). So be careful to reverse (right and left sides) pieces on your marker, as indicated in the illustration.

    Why all the fuss? Because the nap is darker and richer in tone when it is up than when it is down. And if you mix up and have parts of the same garment running in different directions, it will look totally . . . I'm searching for the correct word, and the only one I can find is *weird*.

Fig. 14

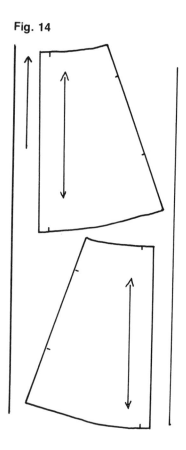

Press on the straight of grain of the fabric, not against it. You can hold the iron parallel to the grain and do a whole garment faster than if you wiggle it all over, creating little "bias" waves. Teach yourself to do this. You can press *across* the grain or *with* the grain—but not on the diagonal!

When sewing, keep the bulk of the fabric to the outside of the machine so that you'll have more freedom to manipulate and maneuver. Of course, there are times when you can't, but as a rule, the bulk should always be to the outside.

*

When sewing seam binding, or lace for a curved hem, hold it under the slightest of tension. This takes up excess fabric, and will make the actual hemming that much easier. Not too tight, now!

*

Fig. 15

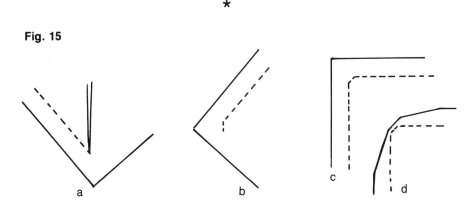

For points, such as those on collars, cuffs, and decorative trim, follow these instructions: Make sure seam allowance is $\frac{1}{4}$ inch. Stitch along seam line until it is almost directly over the point. Lower needle into fabric (Fig. 15a). Raise presser foot, turn fabric on the diagonal, lower presser foot, and sew two stitches across the point, ending once more with needle in fabric and on the $\frac{1}{4}$-inch seam line (Fig. 15b—for the sake of clarity, the needle is not shown in this drawing). Turn fabric once more (Fig. 15c), and continue sewing. Trim close to stitch (Fig. 15d). The point will come out squarer and sharper this way than if you sew it by just turning the corner!

*

On scallops, sew two stitches straight across (Fig. 16a). Cut into corners (Fig. 16b), and trim (Fig. 16c).

Fig. 16

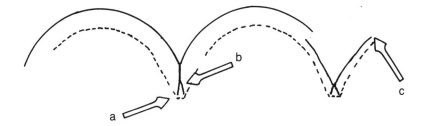

Fig. 17

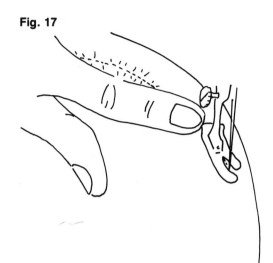

To take in fullness on a regular set-in sleeve, all you have to do is sew with a medium stitch, about ten to an inch, while holding your finger on the fabric behind the presser foot. This way, you are "retarding" the fabric. You will find this gives a rounded shape to the cap of the sleeve and makes setting it in simple (Fig. 17).

Sew with the sleeve side up. Also, there is a tendency to make ends meet (if your gathers aren't quite right) by pulling either the top or bottom to match the other (Fig. 18). *Don't do this!* It gives the set-in sleeve an awkward shape.

As a matter of fact, any time you are sewing a smaller piece to a larger one, or when you are attaching gathers to a flat or ungathered piece, sew with the fuller piece on top, and watch out for pulling!

*

To prepare elastic for the skirts in this book, for sleeves, or for just about anything that is round . . . use a good "hard" elastic. This is often called "webbed" elastic. For skirts, I prefer to use a ¾-inch width, since it is easy to handle and doesn't twist as much as narrower widths.

Fig. 18

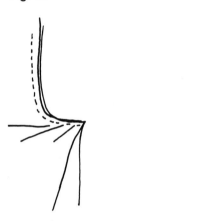

If an elastic waistband is required for your skirt, cut the elastic two inches smaller than your waist. Holding ends together, test to see that it gets around your hips.

Holding the elastic as in Fig. 19, one end half an inch over the other, sew back and forth several times with a small stitch. This will give you a circle of elastic ready to insert into your skirt.

*

An excellent way to put a garment together is in sections. Complete one section or one step at a time, before going on to the next. In this way, if you become tired, or are interrupted, you will be able to go back to where you were with a minimum of confusion. For instance: Prepare *both* sleeves for insertion. Don't do one completely and then the other. Do both cuffs first, then set them onto the sleeve. On skirts where there is a right and left facing, prepare the facings. This will save time too.

Fig. 19

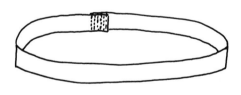

CUTTING TIPS

The patterns included in this book all conform to my standards. They are not like patterns you buy in the store. That is, they are all made with ½-inch seam allowances, and with too many notches. But, too many notches is exactly what I want!

When you buy a commercial pattern, you will find they have a ⅝-inch seam allowance on all seams, even where they need smaller ones! They want you to trim after you sew. Frankly, if a factory worked like that, the cost would be prohibitive—both fabric and time would be wasted.

So, the following tips for the home sewer are based on knowledge gleaned in a factory from pattern makers and cutters. They translate the designer's pattern into as simple a sewing-and-cutting project as possible and prepare the pieces for the operators or seamstresses. The very way they prepare the pattern makes it easier to sew!

Of course, you don't have their cutting equipment, such as the special marking paper, cutting machines that cut through hundreds of garments at a time, hole makers, etc. Or even the gloriously long cutting tables—fifty feet is a short one! But there is no reason why, with confidence in yourself and me, logic, and a careful following of cutting rules and directions, you can't eliminate a lot of useless, time-consuming work.

This section is to me the most valuable in the book. If I can only demystify some of the cutting for you, I will feel that I've made the price of the book worthwhile.

READ INSTRUCTIONS CAREFULLY. For both commercial patterns and the ones enclosed in this book, follow the rule of first reading them over before cutting. Read them over until you understand why the garment is put together the way it is. That way you will minimize the possibility of errors in cutting, as well as in sewing.

FOLLOW CUTTING INSTRUCTIONS. Commercial patterns usually have excellent ones. There are reasons to lay out patterns according to these instructions. Not only will you save fabric, but you are assured that the grain lines will be correct. If the grain is correct, the garment will hang well—or, putting it more simply, the garment will look and feel right.

*

In a factory, the cutter makes a "marker" before cutting. That is, he or she marks out the pattern pieces on a length of paper (the paper is as wide as the fabric to be used, and comes in rolls of a hundred yards), much like a puzzle, or floor plan. The patterns are traced onto the paper using as little paper as possible. The less space (paper) used, the less fabric eventually used. In this way, when all the pieces of a pattern are traced, it will be clear exactly how much fabric will be needed per garment. A marker looks like this (Fig. 20). (The long shaped wrap across grain.) Please note the way notches are indicated on the marker. Both factory professionals and home sewers tend to overlook dots marking holes to be punched (which indicate the bottoms of darts and show where to start buttonholes in these patterns). To prevent this, get into the habit of putting large circles around these dots to call attention to them. You might even draw arrows pointing to them. I've done that myself. If you do not have paper that is large enough, you can even Scotch-tape newspapers together. Once you get used to making a marker, you'll never want to do cutting any other way.

Fig. 20

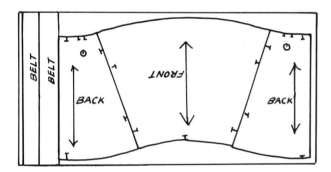

Fig. 21

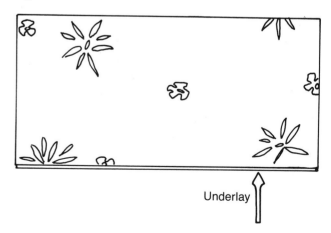

Underlay

Use a T-square to insure a square end on the marker. Mark ½-inch down each side of marker. (Don't use selvage for this allowance, even if a piece is on the straight. Selvages don't "give" in sewing and will pucker.) You will then trace your pattern beginning from this line (as though you were working within a frame).

The extra time it takes to make a marker will often save you the pain of incorrect or incomplete cutting. Try it at least once!

Use a large space to cut. I am a confirmed floor-user. I always put paper—either large sheets of tissue (such as is used for wrapping gifts) or newspaper—down first. Not for cleanliness; I assume your floor is clean. Mine is most of the time. I put the paper down, as the cutter does in the factory, to prevent the fabric from slipping. Paper is *always* placed beneath the fabric in factory cutting, and this paper is called an "underlay." First you make your marker, then you cut the underlay—it should be the same size as the marker, but it need not be marked with the pattern. Your fabric should be laid out on the underlay (Fig. 21), and the marker then placed on top.

Let me review the steps for you. Once you learn them, I feel sure you won't want to cut any other way.

1. Lay out and trace pattern onto paper as wide as fabric you plan on using. (Be sure grains of fabric are correct.) This is the marker.

2. Cut underpaper (underlay) to the same width and length as above.

3. Remove marker and lay out fabric, making sure selvages are straight.

4. Replace marker. Pin through all three thicknesses (marker, fabric, underlay) near corners, notches, and edges of pattern. Don't pin across cutting lines. Weight ends (Fig. 22).

5. Weight each piece. Cut through three thicknesses.

6. Cut notches. If the pattern has darts, mark them.

*

Fig. 22

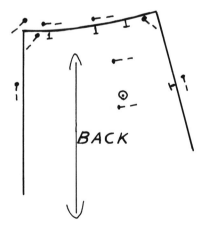

BACK

There are those among you who won't want to do the above, incredible as that seems to me. You have an alternative, and quite good, way of cutting:

1. Study the pattern and directions.

2. Place pattern on top of fabric, following cutting guide. Trace with tailor's chalk.

3. Lay out underpaper to prevent slipping. (The same size as the "marked" fabric.)

Fig. 23

Fig. 24

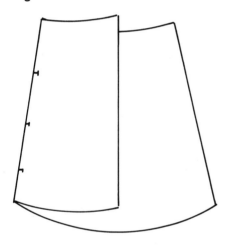

Fig. 25

4. Pin at corners and near notches.
5. Weight and cut.

*

Special weights are used in cutting rooms. At home, lacking these weights, I have discovered the "perfectness" of grapefruits and my daughter's penny collection. An iron, in emergencies, is also excellent. Last time I used one, though, I forgot to empty it of water. Need I say what happened?

*

When cutting notches, they need not be like the top two in Fig. 23—a small slash, like the bottom one, will do the trick just as well. Cut in no more than $\frac{1}{4}$ inch—that's plenty!

Add notches to patterns. As a matter of fact, when you are using a commercial pattern, the first thing you should do is read the pattern instructions. Second, trim seams to $\frac{1}{2}$ inch and $\frac{1}{4}$ inch, following the rules I suggested (see page 5). Third, make notches—more and more of them! But be sure, as in skirt side seams, to lay one piece over the other, making sure side seams are together (Fig. 24), and make a few more notches. You can't have too many, ever. Well, almost ever.

I always add center notches to commercial patterns. These patterns often do not indicate a notch on center neck backs. It really is a great help to have one there, so that the corresponding piece matches easily. You can't have too many notches. That's the second time I've said that. I believe it so much that I want to convince you of it. A notch is like a signpost along a road you've never been on. Although you know where you are going, you may need assurance that you are getting there from time to time.

Add notches to skirt pattern pieces—to center fronts, sides, backs, facings, etc.—and be sure that there is always a corresponding notch on the piece you are joining it to.

When joining two pieces together for a back or front, I always look for a double slash on top. I know then, without even thinking, that it is the center and the top (Fig. 25). Get into the habit of making these double slashes.

*

When making darts, pin around the dart. Use a long needle, and, holding it perpendicular to the fabric, place it through the small circle at the bottom of the dart (Fig. 26). Remove the pattern piece, keeping the needle in position, and mark the point with tailor's chalk on the wrong side of the fabric. Then, again using tailor's chalk, mark on the wrong side from the center hole at bottom to the slashes (notches) at the top, the widest part of the dart (Fig. 27).

In the factory, darts are marked with holes at the bottom, slashes at the top (the operators don't use tailor's chalk). This saves one more step. Experiment and see if you can sew a straight line. Starting from the slashes, sew to the center hole and a little beyond, as discussed previously (page 7).

*

You can, if you choose, use pinking shears to cut out your pattern, though they should not be used to cut around necks or armholes (where you should instead cut a $\frac{1}{4}$-inch seam allowance with regular scissors). Using pinking shears saves time, and the finish of the garment will be better.

*

The last tip of this chapter: Cut when children, friends, dogs, and cats are out of the room—preferably when they are out of the house, and will be so for a while. Good luck! I hope I've helped you.

Fig. 26

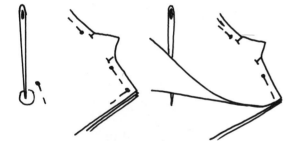

Fig. 27

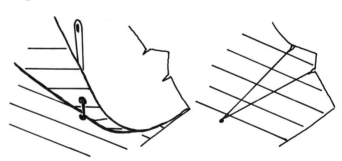

CHAPTER TWO

THE MARVELOUS RECTANGLE

In many ways the rectangle is both the easiest and the most challenging of all pattern shapes. It is, without any doubt, the simplest to sew. Once you get the knack, you can make any number of skirts based on the rectangle within a short amount of time. The challenge comes from the infinite variety, the possibilities the shape offers. In moments of discussion with other sewing enthusiasts, I have counted as many as a dozen different styles we had each made that year, independent of the other, all inspired by the rectangle.

Let's start with the one I made the most often: the wrap. It is easy to wear. It is one of those skirts you put your hand out to grab when you don't know what you feel like wearing. It always feels good. I suppose the reason is that, like our bodies, it expands in the waist.

I've been accused of living in my denim one. I wear it in the summer when I am always at my thinnest, and into the fall and holiday season when I always gain weight. If this section is called "The Marvelous Rectangle," this skirt deserves the name "The Marvelous Wrap."

I own this same style of skirt in several fabrics, in plaids, solids, and prints. Once you master the simple sewing technique, once the logic of the sewing becomes clear to you, I predict this will be the skirt you sit down to make on rainy afternoons!

Fig. 28   Basic long wrap

BASIC LONG WRAP (Fig. 28)

Materials needed

1⅔ yards of 45-inch-wide fabric
1⅔ yards of lining fabric
3½ to 4 yards of 1½-inch grosgrain ribbon

How to sew

Cut the fabric to a perfectly straight 40 × 60 inches.

Cut the lining to a perfectly straight 39 × 60 inches.

With right sides of fabric together (facing each other), sew the lining to the fabric along the bottom edge (Fig. 29).

Then, aligning the skirt and the lining at the top edges, pin side seams (Fig. 30). Sew side seams together.

Turn the fabric right side out, once more aligning top edges, and make running stitches along the top edge through the skirt and lining (Fig. 31).

Fig. 29

Fig. 30

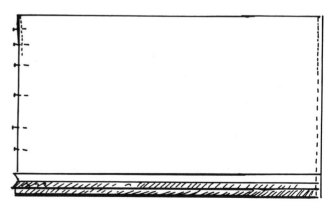

Fig. 31

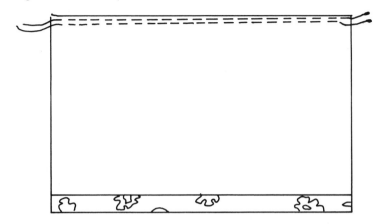

Pull the running stitches to measure 36 inches. Make sure the gathers are even! Mark the center with a pin.

Cut off 37 inches of ribbon. Turn under ½ inch of the ribbon to the front. With lining side up, sew along the bottom of the ribbon, covering and holding the gathered stitches in place (Fig. 32).

Then, taking the balance of the ribbon, mark the center of the piece with a pin, and with the right side of the skirt to you, match center pins (Fig. 33a). Placing ribbon over previously sewn ribbon, topstitch the top edge first, then down the side, along the bottom, and up the other side (Fig. 33b).

If your machine has a buttonhole attachment, make a buttonhole in the center of the waistband (ribbon) for the ties to go through. You don't need to do this, but it does give a more professional look and fit to the garment.

Press and wear!

Variations and general information

Add or subtract in length according to your height. For most women of from 5 feet 3 inches to 5 feet 6 inches, 40 inches seems to be the right length.

For daytime wear, I cut a piece of fabric 29 × 60 inches. This hits me in the middle of my calf. I feel both neat and comfortable in this length skirt.

If you choose not to line a skirt, why, just turn under and stitch the side seams, sew seam binding on the bottom edge, and either hand sew or stitch on machine.

For what I call "glamour" wear, soft drapy fabric, such as nylon, banlon, chiffon, or crepe, looks especially marvelous. I cut

Fig. 32

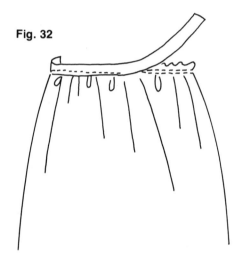

Fig. 33

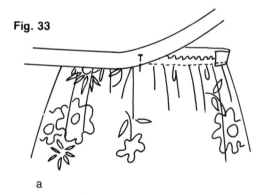

a

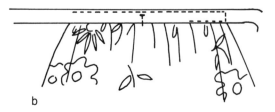

b

the fabric 90 × 40 inches (2½ yards instead of 1⅔ yards) and don't line it. I use a good velvet ribbon for the front band, "picking up" one of the colors in the fabric.

Fig. 34. Ribbon and lace on voile (wonderful for summer).

Fig. 35. Rickrack border.

Fig. 36. Apron look (a success with teenagers).

Fig. 37. Appliqué border (surrounding circles with rickrack).

Fig. 38. The crazy-quilt look (use those old small scraps you've been saving, surround them with narrow black rickrack and you will have a glamorous evening skirt that is timeless). If you have patience, embroider around each piece of fabric, using three strands of embroidery thread.

Fig. 34   Ribbon and lace

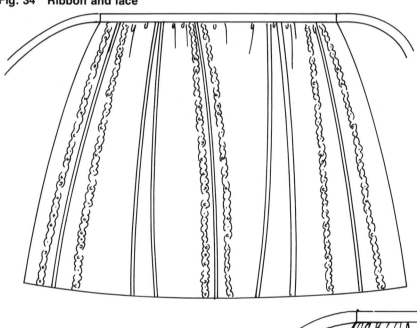

Fig. 35   Rickrack border

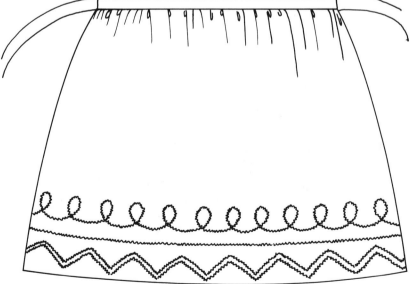

Fig. 36   Apron look

Fig. 37   Appliqué border (surrounding circles in rickrack)

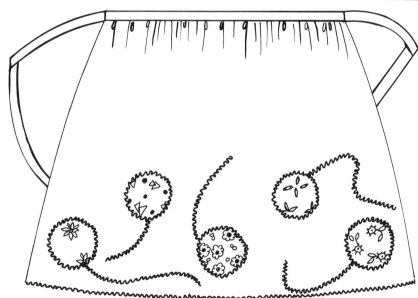

Fig. 38   Crazy quilt

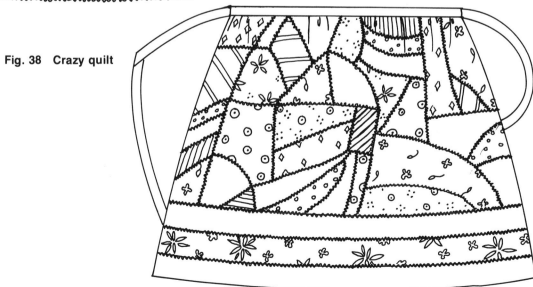

Fig. 39

RUFFLED WRAP (Fig. 39)

Materials needed

2 yards of 45-inch fabric
1½ yards of lining fabric
3½ to 4 yards of 1½-inch grosgrain ribbon

Cutting guide (Fig. 40)

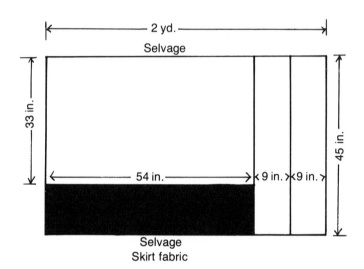

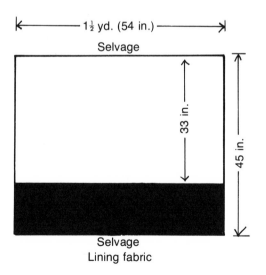

Fig. 40   Ruffled wrap skirt cutting guide

How to sew

Join the ruffle strips together at one end and make a narrow hem on three sides (Figs. 41a, 41b). Make running stitches along free side and gather ruffle to measure 53 inches (Fig. 41c).

With right side of ruffle to right side of fabric, pin along bottom edge, leaving $\frac{1}{2}$-inch space at either end (Fig. 42).

Place lining right over this, edge of lining to edge of fabric, pin, and sew with a $\frac{1}{2}$-inch seam (Fig. 43). Do not "catch" ruffles at sides.

Turn right side out, gather fabric and lining along top edge.

Follow instructions under Basic Long Wrap for belt (Figs. 32, 33a, 33b).

Press and wear!

Fig. 41

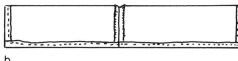

a

b

c

Fig. 42

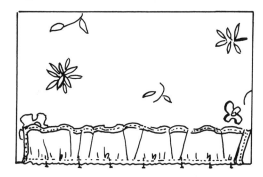

Fig. 43

Variations

This skirt looks wonderful in a soft wool blend. This fabric usually comes in 54-inch and 60-inch widths, so for this skirt you would cut it across the fabric (31 inches) and add the 18 inches for the ruffles. A yard and a half is all you need for this skirt. The lining requires the same amount of fabric: $1\frac{1}{2}$ yards.

I've also made this in two sizes of gingham. I used $1\frac{1}{2}$ yards of the smaller check for the body, and $\frac{1}{2}$ yard of the larger check for the ruffle (Fig. 44).

Fig. 44

Fig. 45

PATCHWORK LONG WRAP (Fig. 45)

This skirt deserves a book by itself! I've had a long history with it. I've made it in printed cottons, in denims, in a wool with solids and woven designs, in satins and corduroys and velvets. There is no end to the list of fabrics and possibilities for this skirt. I sold it to many of the best department stores in the United States, and it's been in catalogues and ads in every fabric and color. Do I have to tell you I love it?

If you are—as are most sewers—a fabric addict, this is the perfect answer to all those odd pieces you simply can't throw away. You can make a mix of fabrics and colors or, as I prefer, make arrangements of "families" of colors, or decide on a two- or three-color combination and stick to it. I've even cut up old denim pants and mixed in alternating patches of denim and bandana cloth. I bought damaged bandanas on sale. Let your imagination go wild, and play with colors and textures. As always, I like to pick out one of the colors in the fabric for the color of the waistband ribbon. And, if I plan a "glamour" patchwork, I use either a satin or velvet ribbon for the top piece. Have fun!

Materials needed

Scraps from your scrap bag of treasures
    or
1 yard each of two fabrics (for a two-fabric combination)
    or
$\frac{2}{3}$ yard each of three fabrics (for a three-fabric combination)
    or
$\frac{1}{2}$ yard each of four fabrics (for a four-fabric combination)
    etc.
$1\frac{1}{2}$ yards of lining fabric (cotton for cottons, rayon for other fabrics)
$3\frac{1}{2}$–4 yards of $1\frac{1}{2}$-inch grosgrain ribbon
1 piece of fabric 4 × 54 inches

Cutting guide

Cut or tear fabric into 7-inch squares. I prefer, even for the home sewer, to cut. You will need fifty-four squares in all: nine strips made up of six 7-inch squares each.

Cut lining fabric into one piece, 39 × 54 inches.

How to sew

The very first thing you must do is decide what overall pattern you want to use. The best way to do this is to lay all the squares on the floor, right side up, and create your "patchwork" pattern. Pick the pieces up in order. The top one on top of the second on top of the third, etc. Whatever system you use, repeat it for all the other strips. Then, when you have nine little bundles before you, pin a number on each one: *1* on bundle 1, *2* on bundle 2, etc., through bundle 9.

Machine sew bundle 1 into strips. Then 2, on through 9. Once more, when all the strips are sewn (I suggest a ½-inch seam), place them on the floor in a row and check that you have not gotten them out of order. This is a lot easier than it sounds!

Then join strip 2 to 1. Strip 3 to 2. Just keep joining the strips in order. When the patchwork is completed, with right sides together, sew the piece of narrow fabric (4 × 54 inches) to the bottom edge (Fig. 46).

Follow instructions used for Basic Long Wrap to complete.

Press and wear!

Fig. 46

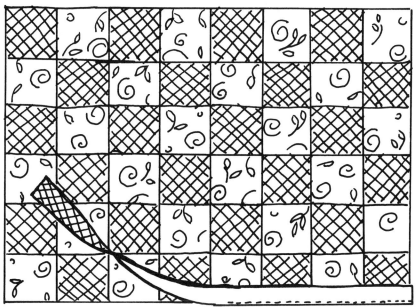

Variations

Fig. 47. Appliqué on squares.

Fig. 48. Diamond pattern using 8-inch squares cut in half diagonally.

Fig. 49. Patch with rickrack outlines.

Fig. 50. Alternating patch and strip.

Fig. 47

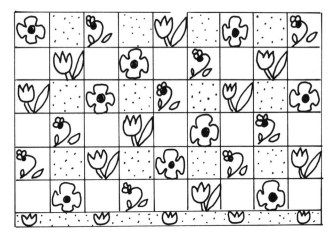

Fig. 48

Fig. 49

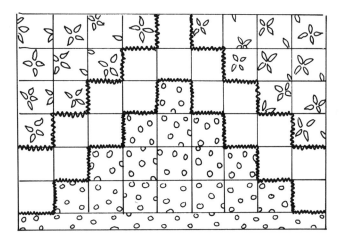

Fig. 50

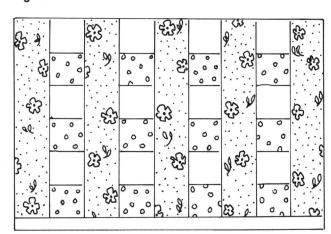

Fig. 51

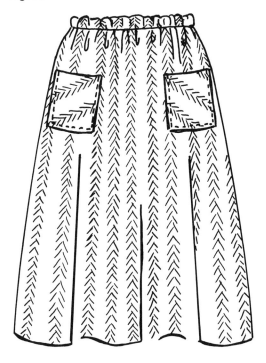

THE ELASTICIZED-WAISTBAND BASIC SKIRT (Fig. 51)

This skirt is amazingly easy to wear. Just one word of caution. If you are very hippy, it just will not fall correctly as is. If you are from size 3–8, this skirt will look and feel good.

Once again, we have a simple-to-sew skirt with infinite variations. It looks good in any slightly heavier than usual cotton fabric. Another way of putting it—go toward the denims, in all colors and textures, woven stripes in cottons, cotton blends, wools, and even cotton knits. Anything, as long as the fabric has body.

Materials needed

$1\frac{1}{3}$ yard of 45-inch-wide fabric for short or long *basic* skirt.
1 yard of $\frac{3}{4}$-inch heavy elastic. (Use the webbed kind, since this has more body than the usual. It can be purchased in any good trimmings store.)

No lining is required unless the fabric is of the sort that will bag. Before it is too late, let me persuade you not to use such fabric for this style.

Fig. 52

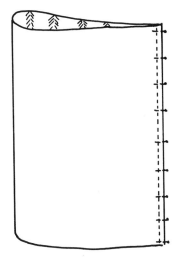

Cutting guide

For short skirt: Cut fabric into a rectangle measuring 31 × 48 inches.

For long skirt: Cut fabric into a rectangle measuring 42 × 48 inches.

How to sew

Pin and then sew down the back center seam (31 inches long for short skirt, 42 inches long for long skirt) with right sides together (Fig. 52). Turn, so that the right side of fabric is out, fold top edge under approximately $\frac{1}{4}$ inch, and sew, making a narrow hem (Fig. 53).

Sew and prepare elastic as discussed in Chapter 1 (see Fig. 19).

Fig. 53

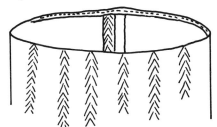

Place elastic on inside of skirt, and fold the top part of the skirt over it. Stitch along narrow hem. Where there is no more room to sew, put needle into fabric to hold it in place (Fig. 54), and pull the elastic toward you—moving gathers along and away. This is easier than it sounds, and, once the garment is in your hand, it will become logical to you.

Even gathers, and stitch on the center back line so that the elastic won't twist (Fig. 55). Find the center front by making sure the gathers are even, and stitch across the elastic there.

Use seam binding and turn up a 1-inch hem, or make a rolled hem using your sewing machine attachment.

Press and wear!

Fig. 54

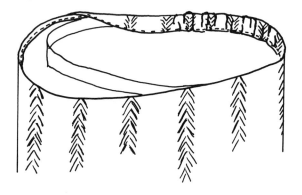

Fig. 55

TIERED SKIRT (Fig. 56)

Fig. 56

I always think of this skirt in relation to Spanish dancing, although it is one of the timeless and flattering skirts women will always wear. The three tiers of graduated gathers is so very graceful that it gives a look of height and grace to even a short woman.

Recently I saw a very striking woman wearing this skirt made up of three very small and different floral prints (see Variations). Yes, I asked her if she had made it. And no, she hadn't. She had bought it in southern France two years before. Each print was on a black background. Most unusual!

Materials needed

2½ yards of 45-inch fabric
1 yard of ¾-inch elastic
6 yards of wide rickrack or narrow ribbon in
contrasting color (optional)

Cutting guide (Fig. 57)

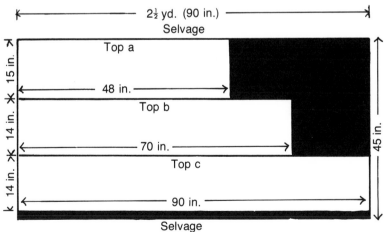

Fig. 57 Tiered skirt cutting guide

How to sew

Gather top edge of section B to 48 inches.

With right sides together, pin and stitch TOP of section B to BOTTOM of section A (Fig. 58).

Gather top edge of section C to 70 inches. Pin and stitch to bottom of section B (Fig. 59).

On right side, sew rickrack over the two seam lines you have just created (Fig. 60).

With right sides together, pin back seams together—matching seam lines and rickrack, and stitch from the top down. Seams should go up (see Fig. 61).

Follow instructions for Elasticized-Waistband Basic Skirt to complete. See pages 27 and 28, Figs. 53–55.

Turn to right side and sew rickrack along the very bottom of the skirt (Fig. 62). Turn under raw edge of rickrack at ends as you backtack.

Press and wear!

Fig. 58

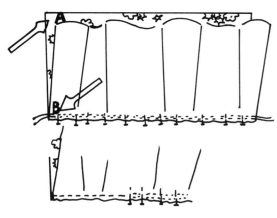

Fig. 59

Fig. 60

Fig. 61

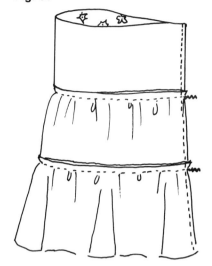

Fig. 62

Variations and general chitchat

Floral prints in large patterns just don't seem to look good in this style. You can either use three different small prints, as long as they are all the same background color, or all the same print. Light colors also don't look good in prints in this style. Stick to the darker tones for an unusual skirt. For holiday wear, try one of these in a good quality satin-back crepe, the kind that is soft and drapy, not the stiff satin. Omit the rickrack on the crepe skirt, and invest in a small extra amount of fabric for a wide sash. With a simple long-sleeved blouse and a small amount of jewelry, this skirt is suited to the most formal occasions.

CHAPTER THREE

THE SHAPED WRAP

This wrap has the quality of disguise. It makes the too thin person look graceful and the too heavy person look willowy. It expands with your waist.

I've made this skirt in fabrics as diverse as wool tweeds and polished cottons. I don't think there is a fabric that wouldn't look good in this style. A few summers ago, I did a collection using East Indian cotton prints. I've also made this skirt from East Indian bedspreads, using the border for the overlap in the back. *Or* in the front. For, you see, you can wear this skirt either way.

I suggest you make two copies of this pattern (which is among those included in the back of the book): one in the short version, one in the long. You should also make copies of the extra pieces needed for the long and short dirndl. You may well be using them the rest of your life, so trace the patterns onto a good sturdy paper (see Fig. 80, page 39).

For those of you with less than perfect shapes (like me) I suggest that you make the wrap with darts and/or plackets. *Read the sections about these (pages 47 and 48) before you make any of the other shaped wraps. Then, if you choose, apply the darts or plackets to the other styles! (See Figs. 99–107.)*

BASIC SHORT AND LONG WRAP— WITHOUT DARTS (Fig. 63)

Fig. 63

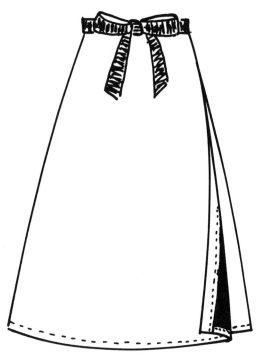

Materials needed for short wrap
Straight of goods with self belt: 2¼ yards of 45-inch goods
Across grain with self belt: 2 yards of 45-inch goods

Materials needed for long wrap
Across grain with self belt: 2⅔ yards of 45-inch goods

Cutting guide
Short basic wrap (Fig. 64)

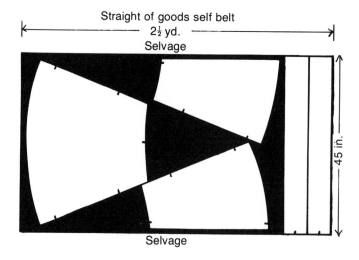

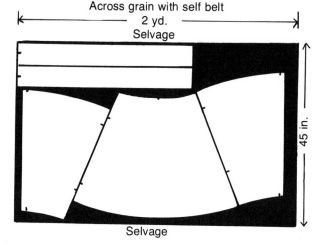

Fig. 64   Short basic wrap cutting guides

Long basic wrap (Fig. 65)

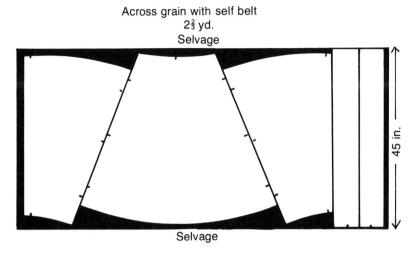

Fig. 65   Long basic wrap cutting guide

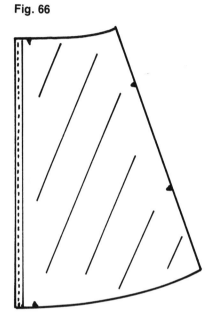

Fig. 66

Fig. 67

How to sew

On both back pieces, turn under $\frac{1}{4}$ inch on self facings and stitch (Fig. 66).

Turn self facing at notches (top and bottom), with right sides together, and stitch 1-inch seam along bottom only (Fig. 67).

Turn so that wrong sides face each other, and stitch facing down at top (Fig. 68). Your back pieces are now ready to be joined to the center front.

With right sides together, and notches matching, join side pieces to front. Sew from the top to the bottom (Fig. 69).

Fig. 68

Fig. 69

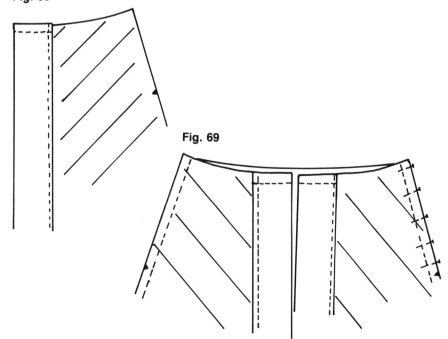

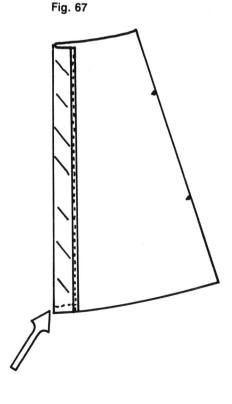

Starting at the right top, with the inside of the garment facing you (Fig. 70), stitch down the facing, going over previous stitching line until about 1 inch from bottom.

Turn under raw edge, beginning under the facing, to about $\frac{1}{2}$ inch, and stitch along bottom (Fig. 71), making hem. Stitch up other side.

SELF BELT: Join the two 45–inch pieces of fabric at one end (Fig. 72).

Notch 19 inches from center seams on top and bottom on both sides (Fig. 73).

With right sides together, sew from notches to ends of belt and across. You can sew it straight at the ends, or at an angle. I prefer an angle. Trim off excess fabric on ends (Fig. 74).

Turn sewn belt sections to right side (Fig. 75).

Fig. 70

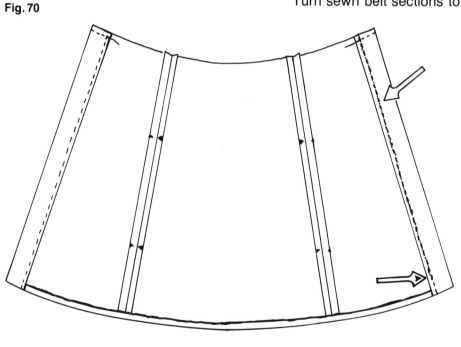

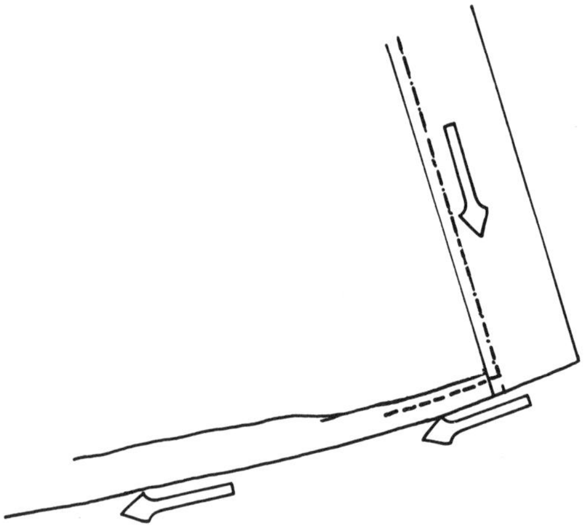

Fig. 71

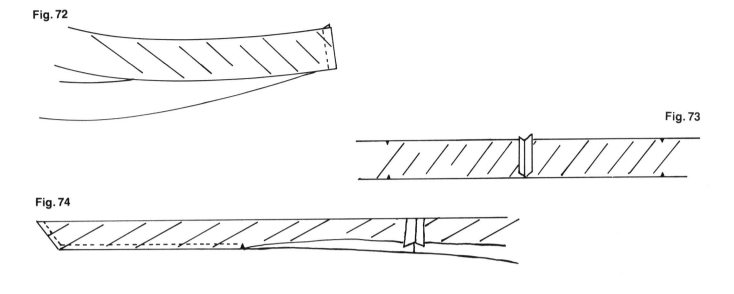

Fig. 72

Fig. 73

Fig. 74

Fig. 75

With edges together, and center seams on center notch of skirt front, place right side of belt to wrong side of skirt. Pin, then stitch, with the belt side up (Fig. 76). Be sure you don't stretch the skirt: Ease as you sew. Don't catch loose side of belt (see arrow in drawing).

If you find ends or centers don't match, adjust the belt. If it is too long, sew it a little more in the center. If the belt is too short, open it up on the sides. Just be sure to renotch the ends if you open it up on the ends.

Fig. 76

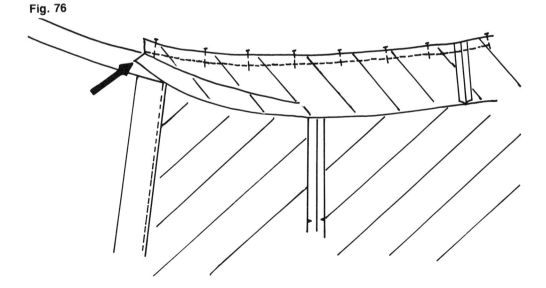

Turn under the seam allowance on front of belt (Fig. 77a), and stitch close to the edge over seam lines (Fig. 77b).

Be sure the back of the belt doesn't roll over, but stays flat. Keep slipping your hand under the fabric to check. Remember to backtack beginning and end.

This next step is not essential, but I always do it: Stitch along the bottom of the belt, up the side, along the top, and down the other side (Fig. 78). The belt is stronger this way, and the life of the skirt is increased.

Make a buttonhole in the belt. You can set the buttonhole at an angle, or straight up and down, but do not set it horizontally (Fig. 79).

Press and wear!

Fig. 77

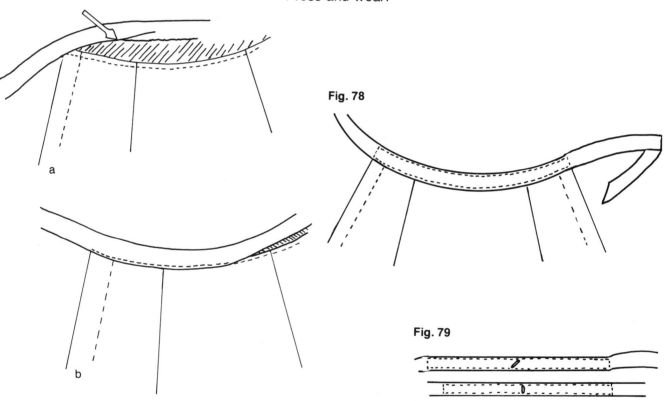

Fig. 78

Fig. 79

General information for making pattern changes

The enclosed pattern is for a midcalf-length skirt. If you want it shorter, cut pattern evenly from the bottom up. The length of the pattern is fashionable now. However, I recently found a picture of myself in exactly the same length skirt. I looked so young and my husband looked so young that I turned the photo over to see if there was a date on the back. There was: June 1954!

The standard length for a long skirt is approximately 42 inches. So, if you want to make a long skirt, add 11 inches to the enclosed pattern. The technique for lengthening one back pattern piece is illustrated in Fig. 80. If you are exceptionally tall or short, make further adjustments to suit your height. Be sure to mark evenly from bottom line, weighting the pattern so that it does not shift. Add extra notches on side seams!

Fig. 80

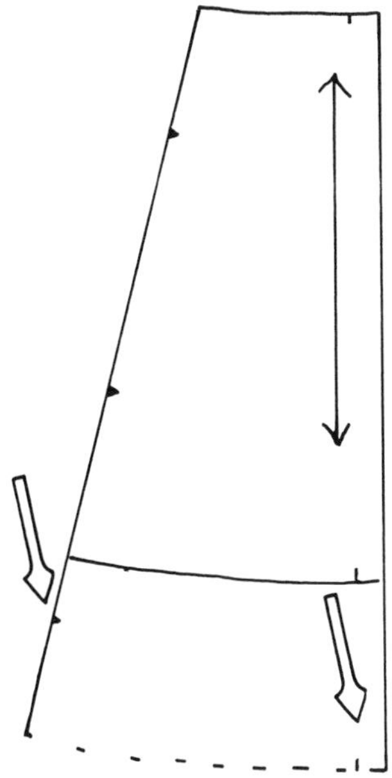

WRAP WITH POCKETS (Fig. 81)

Materials needed

Same as basic wrap (page 34)

Cutting guide

Same as for basic wrap, but with this difference: The pockets and facings come out of the spaces between the main pattern pieces. Be sure to have straight of goods correct! If you don't, the pocket will be at war with the skirt, pulling against it.

How to sew

Turn under $\frac{1}{4}$ inch on pocket facing, so that wrong sides are together (Fig. 82).

Fig. 81

Fig. 82

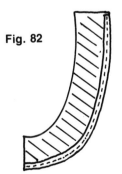

Fig. 83

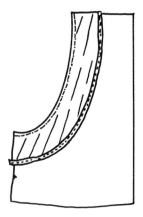

With right side of facing to right side of pocket, stitch $\frac{1}{4}$ inch from the edge (Fig. 83), using a fairly small stitch.

Turn facing to wrong side, and topstitch on right side (Fig. 84).

With notches aligned at side, pin pocket to top and side.

Sew pocket to skirt, sewing from top to bottom of pocket and across bottom to side, turning under $\frac{1}{2}$ inch.

Prepare back sections as in Figs. 66–68.

Join prepared back sections to front (Fig. 85), aligning notches.

Complete as for basic wrap (Figs. 70–79).

Press and wear!

Fig. 84

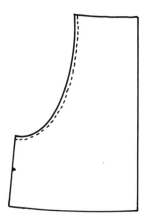

Fig. 85

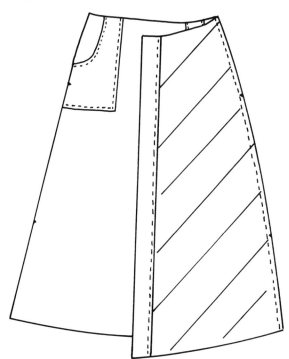

BASIC RUFFLED WRAP (LONG) (Fig. 86)

Fig. 86

Materials needed

Same as for short wrap, plus 1¼ yards.

   (Example: If you want to make the straight of goods with self belt, you will need 3½ yards of 45-inch goods.)

Cutting guide

   Same as basic wrap, *but* you add four 11 × 45-inch strips at one end of marker or fabric (Fig. 87). I hope you've become converted to the marker.

How to sew

   Turn under ¼ inch on back self facing and stitch.

   Join back pieces to front, aligning side seam notches.

   Join the four ruffle strips together, making one long piece (Fig. 88).

   Make a narrow hem on three sides, and sew with seams open and flat (Fig. 89).

Fig. 87   Long ruffled wrap cutting guide

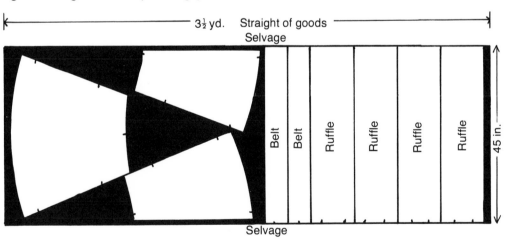

Fig. 88

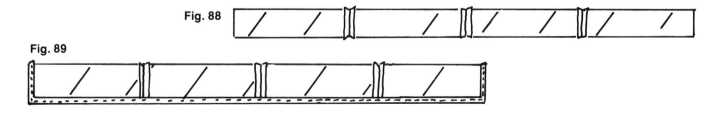

Fig. 89

Gather to approximately 88 inches. Do the gathers in sections, as described in Chapter 1.

Fold over bottom of center piece, finding center, and make a notch.

Starting at back bottom self facing notch (with right sides together and ruffle up), pin every 12 or so inches, matching center seam of ruffle to center notch, and ending at side self facing notch (Fig. 90).

Fold self facing over ruffle and pin (Fig. 91).

Stitch across self facings and over ruffles to other side (Fig. 92). Be sure to backtack.

Fig. 90

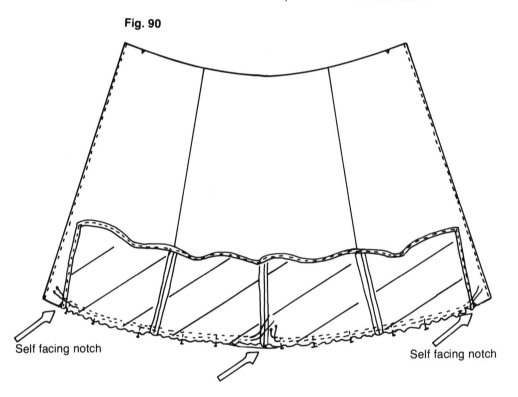

Self facing notch

Self facing notch

Fig. 91

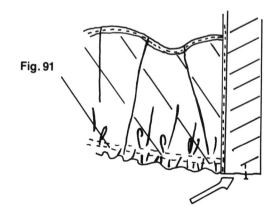

Fig. 92

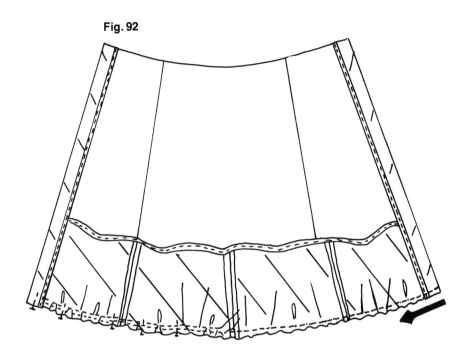

Turn self facing to the wrong side, and complete as for basic wrap (stitching down self facings, across bottom, and up other side). See Figs. 70–79.

Press and wear!

Comments and variations

Make a double ruffle of contrasting fabrics. Cut one 8 inches, the other 11. You can cut more of one than the other if you wish to have extra fullness. Because you will have double bulk, use lightweight fabrics (Fig. 93).

Gather each piece separately, so that the ruffles will fall differently, giving a luxuriant look (Fig. 94).

When cutting original wrap, cut off 11 inches (do this on your marker to save fabric!) and add the ruffles to this shorter skirt for daytime wear.

Fig. 93

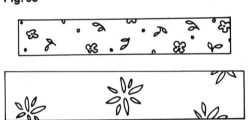

Fig. 94

REVERSIBLE SHAPED WRAP WITH AND WITHOUT CONTRASTING BINDING
(Fig. 95)

Fig. 95

Materials needed for long skirt

With ribbon belt: Two pieces of contrasting fabric, each $2\frac{1}{4}$ yards of 45-inch goods

With self belt: Two pieces of contrasting fabric, each $2\frac{2}{3}$ yards of 45-inch goods

Binding: 6 yards of bias tape, or *true bias* strips joined together as in Fig. 96

Materials needed for short skirt

Straight of goods with self belt: Two pieces of contrasting fabric, each $2\frac{1}{4}$ yards of 45-inch goods

Straight of goods with ribbon belt: Two pieces of contrasting fabric, each 2 yards of 45-inch goods

Across grain with self belt: Two pieces of contrasting fabric, each 2 yards of 45-inch goods

Across grain with ribbon belt: Two pieces of contrasting fabric, each $1\frac{3}{4}$ yards of 45-inch goods

Binding: 5 yards of bias tape, or *true bias* strips joined together as in Fig. 96

Cutting guide

Same as for basic shaped wrap . . . cutting two layers at once.

Fig. 96

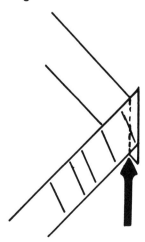

How to sew without binding

Ignore top and bottom notches on back facing. Join backs to front at side seams, aligning notches. Do this for both inside and outside skirt.

Find center on bottom front, and notch on both inside and outside skirt.

Press seams open on both skirts. *You must press now!*

With right sides together, sew from back top down, using a $\frac{1}{2}$-inch seam, turn corner at bottom, and stitch along bottom, aligning side seams and center front notches. Then sew around corner and up the back.

Trim corners.

Turn to right side. Using a heavy pin or needle, push out corners.

Topstitch from top down, along bottom, and up other side. You can stitch any width, as long as it keeps the edges sewn . . . from $\frac{1}{8}$ to $\frac{3}{8}$ inches. You can do a double row of top-stitching if you choose (Fig. 97).

Make adjustment on belt (it will be approximately 3 inches too small, so move notches back $1\frac{1}{2}$ inches on each side), and sew belt.

For ribbon belt, remember to add that extra 3 inches for the back of the belt (see Fig. 32). For self belt, see Figs. 72–79.

Press and wear!

Fig. 97

*

How to sew with binding

Join backs to front at side seams, aligning notches.

Press seams open on both inside and outside skirt. *You must press now!*

Find center on bottom front, and notch on both skirts.

Fig. 98

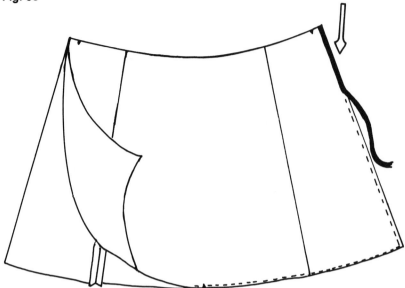

With *wrong sides together*, sew $\frac{1}{4}$ inch from edge down back, along bottom, and up back. Align seams and notches.

Apply binding (Fig. 98).

Make adjustment on belt (it will be approximately 3 inches too small, so move notches back $1\frac{1}{2}$ inches on each side), and sew belt.

For ribbon belt, add an extra 3 inches for the back (see Fig. 32).

Press and wear!

*

The following four skirts can be made up in *any style* in this section. They are to be used for perfecting fit. For instance, in order to assure a particularly well-fitting skirt, you may wish to combine the Wrap with Darts and the Wrap with Plackets for Extra Overlap.

WRAP WITH DARTS (Fig. 99)

Materials needed
Same as for long or short wrap

Cutting guide
Same as for basic long or short wrap (Figs. 64, 65)

How to sew
Sew the same as for basic wrap, but do not put on the belt. Instead, fold over top back edge, aligning notches, and sew from widest part to nothing at bottom (Fig. 100).

Now try on wrap (without belt), pin it closed, and check the fit. This addition of a dart makes an especially good skirt for a body with an extreme difference between waist and hip size.

Darts can be added to the front. Place them in the center and halfway between the center and the side seam . . . or just at those halfway points. Make these darts less than $\frac{1}{2}$ inch at the widest part (Fig. 101). Experiment to see how many darts suit you, and where they should best be placed.

Fig. 99

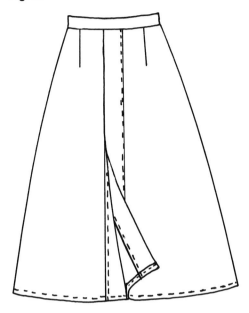

Fig. 100

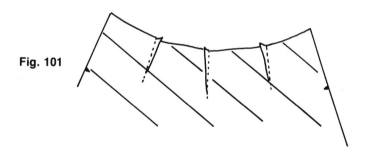

Fig. 101

One advantage of this experimentation is that you need not accept the fit of a ready-made skirt. Just remember to try on your skirt, pin it closed at the top, and look. Look carefully. And, wear the kind of shoes you plan to wear with the skirt. Heel heights *do* make a difference in the hang of a garment.

Complete as in basic wrap, remembering that, if you have taken in an inch of darts, you will have to adjust the belt accordingly. I suggest taking in the belt at the center front seam (Fig. 102). In this case, since you are sewing two pieces take in $\frac{1}{2}$ inch on each—to equal 1 inch.

Sew on belt.

Press and wear!

Fig. 102

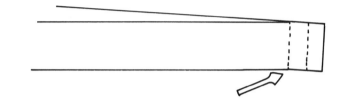

WRAP WITH PLACKETS FOR EXTRA OVERLAP (Fig. 103)

Fig. 103

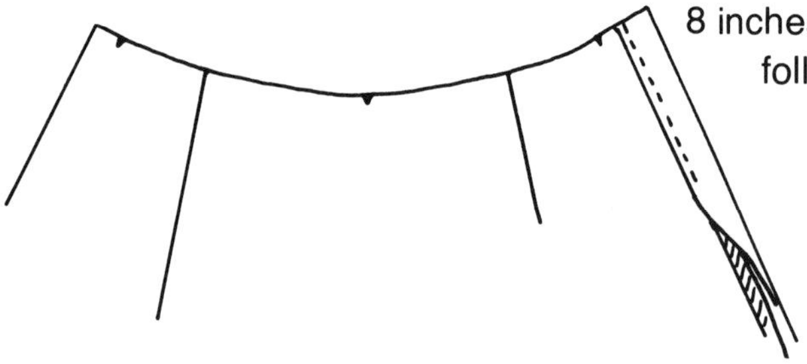

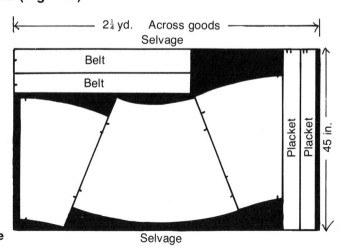

Materials needed

8 inches more of fabric than indicated for any of the skirts shown, following short or long wrap across-grain figures.

Cutting guide (Fig. 104)

Fig. 104   Wrap with plackets cutting guide

Fig. 105

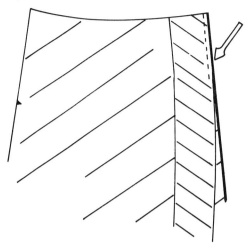

How to sew

Ignore notches on top and bottom of back pieces.

With right side of placket to wrong side of skirt back, sew ½-inch seam down back from top to bottom. Sew both back pieces (Fig. 105).

Fold under ½ inch on placket, turn to front, and, covering stitch, topstitch down placket (Fig. 106).

Join back pieces to front piece at side seams, aligning notches.

Turn under ½-inch hem across bottom of skirt, or, if this should be too bulky for the fabric you have chosen, sew seam binding or lace to hem, and then machine stitch or hand sew hem.

Make adjustment on belt to allow for placket, this time at the side notches (Fig. 107).

Sew belt as for basic wrap.

Press and wear!

Fig. 106

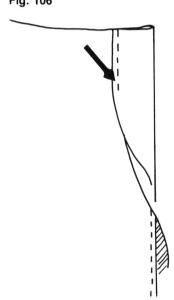

Fig. 107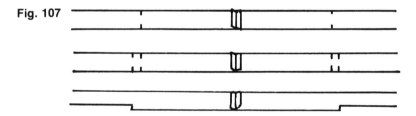

TO LINE THE SHAPED WRAP

There are several ways to line garments, but each garment demands a particular kind of lining. Unfortunately, there are as many rules as there are kinds of fabrics and styles. However, I prefer the two following methods for this particular skirt.

Method 1: Lining as backing

I like this method for sheer cottons. Be sure to use a lining fabric that can be cleaned in the same way as your skirt fabric. If they are to be washed, prewash both before cutting, or make sure they have the same percent of shrinkage allowance. The ends of fabric bolts indicate the shrinkage information.

*

Cut the backs and front of lining at the same time you cut the body of the skirt.

Sew with fairly large stitches (about 8 to an inch) and, with wrong sides of fabric facing each other, sew around each piece (Figs. 108a, 108b). Proceed with skirt as though the two pieces of fabric were one. This is especially useful for fabrics that tend to slide.

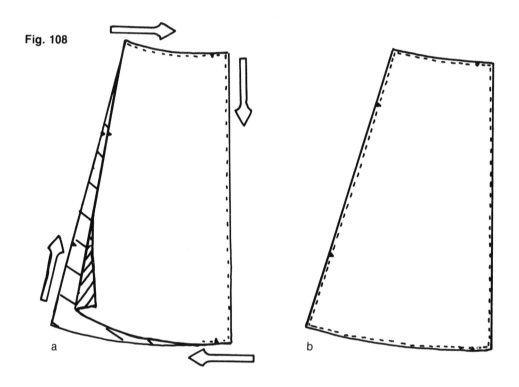

Fig. 108

a   b

Method 2: The free-swinging lining

This is good for all fabrics. I always employ this method for wool skirts, using a lightweight taffeta lining.

*

Cut the two back pieces and the front piece of lining fabric separately from the skirt body. Cut the lining 2 inches shorter than the skirt pattern if you plan on a 1-inch skirt hem. A lining should finish 1 inch shorter than the skirt.

Join lining front piece to back pieces at side seams, aligning notches.

Sew a narrow hem across bottom of lining.

Press seams open and press hem. Put lining aside for the moment.

Sew back pieces of skirt body to front piece at side seams, aligning notches.

Press seams open!

With right side of lining to right side of skirt, sew a ½-inch seam down skirt backs (Fig. 109), joining lining to skirt.

Turn to right side, so that wrong sides face each other.

Make hem on skirt body, turning under, and hand sewing the small amount of unfinished side edge (Fig. 110).

Stitch top of skirt and lining together, matching seams.

Add belt.

Press and wear!

Fig. 109

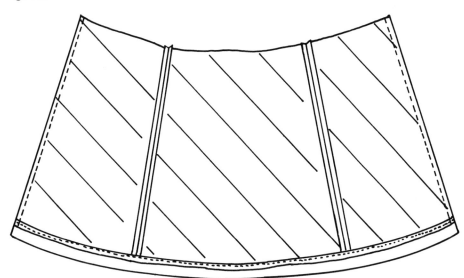

Fig. 110

BASIC DIRNDL WRAP (Fig. 111)

Materials needed

Short dirndl: Across grain with self belt, 3¼ yards of 45-inch goods
Long dirndl: Across grain with self belt, 4 yards of 45-inch goods

Cutting guide

Short dirndl: Fig. 112a
Long dirndl: Fig. 112b

How to sew

This skirt is almost the same as the basic wrap, with two differences. The first is that you cut *two* center pieces. These are then joined together and treated as one. The second difference is that, once all seams are joined and the skirt is hemmed (Figs. 66–71), you will gather the top.

Follow instructions for applying a self belt (Figs. 72–79).

Press and wear!

Variations

If you want a single ruffle on this skirt, follow instructions for ruffled wrap. If you want a double ruffle, see Figs. 93–94.

Fig. 111

Fig. 112 Short and long dirndl wrap cutting guide

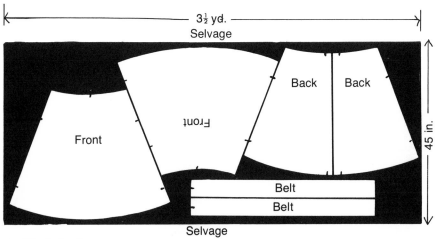

a   Short dirndl wrap

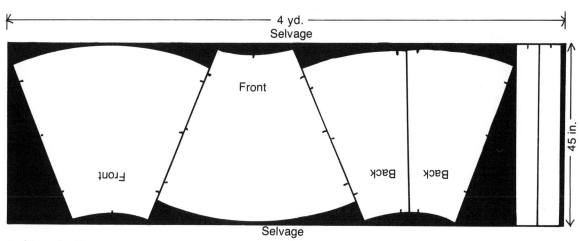

b   Long dirndl wrap

CHAPTER FOUR

THE SHAPED PATCHWORK SKIRT

This skirt is another of my favorites. The fit is slenderizing, and it gives you the chance to use up old pieces of fabric that are too small for a garment and too big to throw out.

I had a great commercial success with this skirt in cotton prints, wool tweeds, and denims. At the time of this writing, there is a craze for thirties and forties clothes. So, I bought some really old dresses for under a dollar in a thrift shop, cut them up into patches, and made an "antique look" skirt. I don't think there is a fabric this skirt would look bad in.

There are some rules to follow though: be sure that all fabrics you use, if the skirt is to be washed, are of the same "shrinkability." If you have old fabric in the house, and want to use it, wash it first, press it, and then cut it out. If you don't do this, you may find that, although all your fabrics are cottons, they shrink at a different rate and leave puckers at the seams. So do the washing first!

I've combined such diverse fabrics as wool tweeds and corduroy for a great-looking result. The tweeds were shades of gray and the corduroy was red. Of course, I made sure all the corduroy nap was "up" (see page 8) . . . just another little warning.

East Indian print bedspreads look terrific cut up into this skirt. For one version I used the bedspread border for the strips and as an "accent," I also put some of the border print on the blouse I made to go with the skirt.

Another great look is a cotton calico combined with gingham. I have used assorted yellow calicos for the patches, and a small orange gingham for the strips and belt. There is no end to the variations possible!

The shape of the skirt lends itself very well to clinging fabrics, such as crepes and soft silks. Try some darker tones for evening wear.

You should fool around with textures and colors that appeal to you particularly. Be the designer. Be brave. I can only give you a few clues, such as: try to keep the colors in the same family, and keep the tones even. By tones I mean depth of color . . . for instance, don't put a very dark tone next to a light

Fig. 113

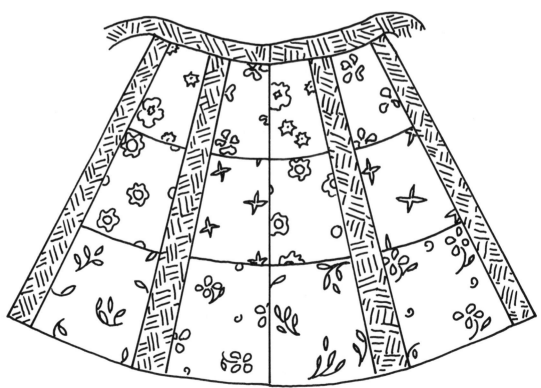

Fig. 114

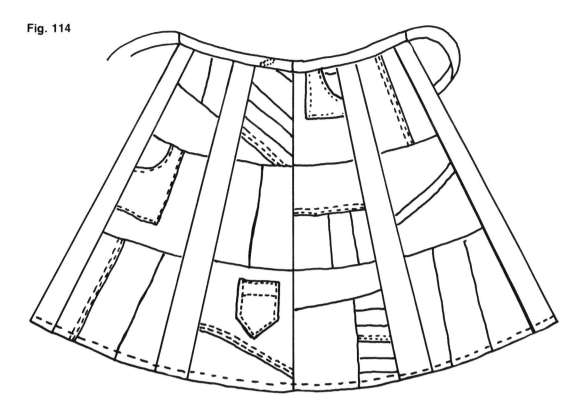

one—one color will overpower the other. But *do* allow for some
sort of contrast in the strips (Fig. 113).

   If you have a group of outgrown or worn-out denim pants,
cut off the legs and use them for the patches and strips. You can
even use the leg seams as "interest" (Fig. 114). If you are daring,
use jeans pockets as patches!

   Experiment and have fun!

SHAPED PATCHWORK SKIRT

Fabric requirements

Because this skirt is always done in combinations, I've broken
down the amounts of fabric needed—for patches, strips, and
belt—and I've also supplied the amount needed for the whole
skirt. If you plan to use two fabrics for the patches, and the amount
required is 55 inches, divide the amount in two, but add a few
inches . . . . Once more, I suggest you make a marker, it's the
little extra work that will ultimately save enormous amounts of
time and, to be dramatic, anguish.

Materials needed for short skirt

Total fabric needed for skirt: 73 inches ($2\frac{1}{4}$ yards) of 45-inch goods

The above amount is with *and* across grain

Across grain—patches and belt: 55 inches (1 inch more than $1\frac{1}{2}$ yards) of 45-inch goods

Across grain—strips only: 19 inches (1 inch more than $\frac{1}{2}$ yard) of 45-inch goods

or

Scraps and new fabric

or

Scraps

Materials needed for long skirt

With grain only (won't fit across grain): Total skirt requires 6 inches less than 4 yards of 45-inch goods

Patches and belt: 92 inches ($2\frac{2}{3}$ yards) of 45-inch goods

Strips: 45 inches ($1\frac{1}{4}$ yards) of 45-inch goods

or

Scraps and new fabric

or

Scraps

Cutting guide

Short skirt: Figs. 115a, 115b

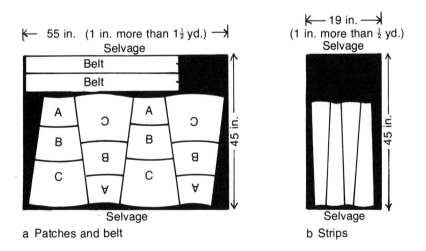

a Patches and belt   b Strips

Fig. 115   Short shaped patchwork cutting guide

Long skirt: Figs. 116a, 116b

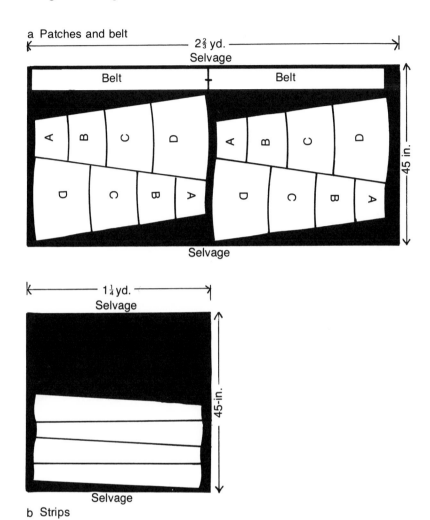

a Patches and belt

b Strips

Fig. 116 Long skirt cutting guide

How to sew short and long skirt

This skirt is the exception to the rule—it is sewn using a $\frac{3}{8}$-inch seam: $\frac{1}{4}$ inch is too little, and $\frac{1}{2}$ inch too much. A $\frac{3}{8}$-inch seam is just between the two and is just right.

The specific directions given here are for the short version. The only difference in the long one is that it calls for a fourth patch (see D on the enclosed pattern for this skirt).

Lay out patches on floor or table so that you can see the skirt as a whole.

Fig. 117

Starting at the left, place largest patch (C) on bottom and place others on top of it, ending with the smallest patch (A). Mark this row number *1*.

Do the same to the other three rows of patches, numbering them 2, 3, and 4. You now have four rows (Fig. 117).

Keep strips separate.

Beginning with row 1, join the smallest piece (A) to the next size (B). With right sides together, place the bottom of patch A on top of patch B. Join them with a ⅜-inch seam, being careful to *ease* them together—*don't* stretch the smaller patch to make it fit.

Fig. 118

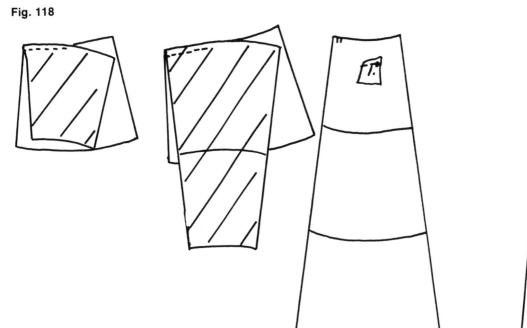

Fig. 119

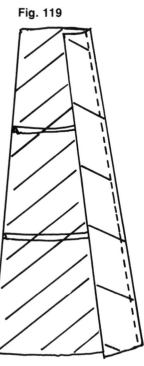

Join the bottom of B to the top of C, with right sides together.

With the right side up, notch the upper left-hand corner (Fig. 118).

Take one strip, and, with the right side of the strip to the wrong side of the joined row 1, on the side you have notched, sew a seam from top to bottom, sewing over seams on patches so that they face down (Fig. 119).

Turn under $\frac{3}{8}$-inch seam on raw side of strip and turn to the front, and, covering stitch, topstitch down (Fig. 120). (Be careful, the strip is slightly on the bias. Don't stretch it!) Align notches as always.

Stitch second strip to this section (Fig. 121), right sides together.

Join second row of patches. Stitch this row to strip on previously sewn section (Fig. 122).

Fig. 120

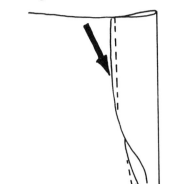

Fig. 121

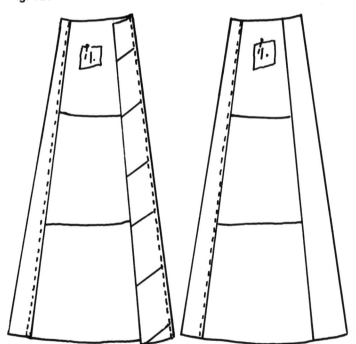

Fig. 122

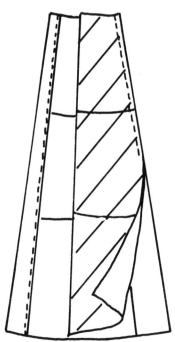

Join third row of patches, and stitch this to second row (Fig. 123).

Stitch third strip to row 3 (Fig. 124).

Join fourth row of patches.

With right sides together, stitch to third strip (Fig. 125).

Stitch last strip, with right side of strip to wrong side of patches, from the top to the bottom.

Turn under seam allowance, and turn to right side and top-stitch over previous stitching. (This is a repeat of Figs. 119 and 120.)

Make hem.

Press and wear!

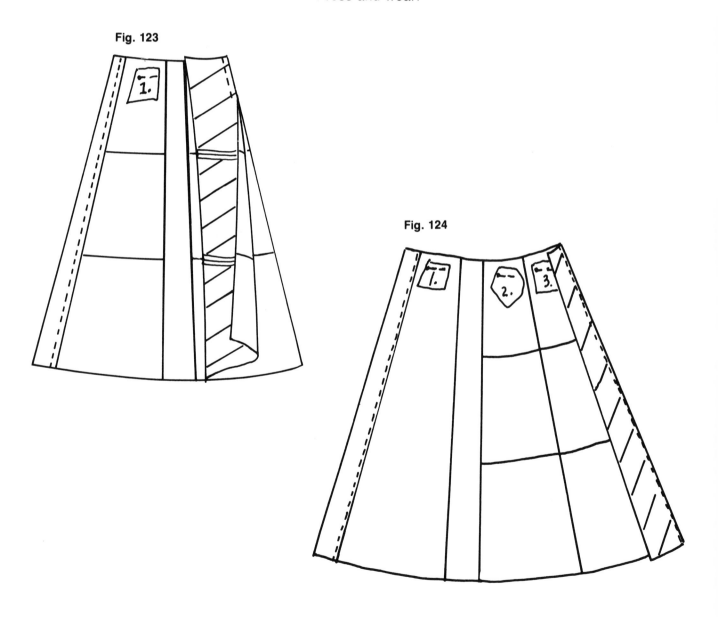

Fig. 123

Fig. 124

Fig. 125

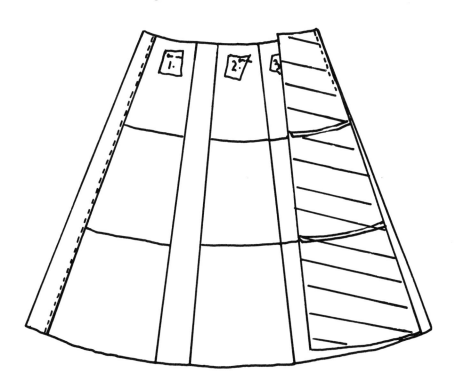

CHAPTER FIVE

THE GORE SKIRT

This is my version of the gore skirt. Once more I find myself telling you that a skirt is easy to sew and wear, flattering to all sizes, and slimming.

I've made it in cottons and wools, in heavy and sheer fabrics. Naturally, the long version of this skirt is well suited for evening wear, and the short one is too, particularly if you make it up in a glamour fabric. I have made it in silks, crepes, and a satin-back crepe, with the satin side up. It looked gorgeous. I confess I've never made it in velvets, although I suspect it would look marvelous that way too.

You can make it in one, two, or three different patterned fabrics, right on up to a different pattern for each gore in the skirt. Just try to keep the color values the same—you don't want one or two colors popping out at you. Also, keep the fabric weights and the kind of fabric the same. A heavy fabric sewn to a light one will create "waves" at worst, ripples at best.

Fig. 126

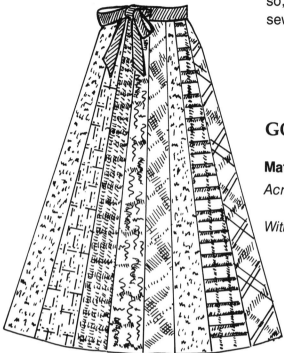

Don't use a knit. The seams in this skirt are all on the bias, so, because of their stretchiness, using knits would turn a simple sewing project into a chore.

GORE SKIRT AS A WRAP (Fig. 126)

Materials needed for short skirt

Across grain: Two pieces, 50 inches each, of 45-inch fabric (a total of 100 inches)

With the grain: This is only possible in either one fabric, or three . . . unless you don't mind wasting fabric. You get seven pieces going from selvage to selvage . . . and all you need is sixteen pieces. Of course, you do get extra patch pieces to use in the future . . . Three pieces, 30 inches each, of 45-inch fabric (90 inches total). The belt is made up of pieces of the three fabrics. I really don't advise that you do it this way, but if you already have the fabric around the house, and want to use it up . . . well, fine, go ahead.

Lining (across grain only): $2\frac{1}{2}$ yards

Materials needed for long skirt

Across grain: Two pieces, 72 inches each, of 45-inch fabric (144 inches total)

Lining (across grain only): $3\frac{1}{4}$ yards

Additional material information

If you want to make this skirt in more than two fabrics, please make a marker first, indicating on it the number of pieces you will use in each fabric. All you will need is one marker, but, for instance, if you want the skirt to be done in four pieces each of four fabrics, get the correct amount you will need for those four pieces! See the marker section in the first chapter and Fig. 20.

Making a lining pattern

There is no lining pattern included in this book. However, it is a simple matter to make one for this skirt. Trust me, and do it.

Sew eight pieces together using $\frac{3}{8}$-inch seams. Press carefully.

Fig. 127

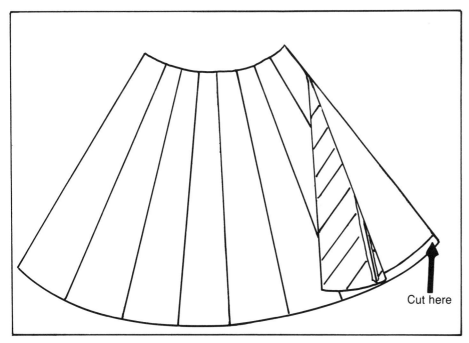

Cut here

Place sewn fabric on top of heavy paper, and trace outline. Cut the traced outline 2 inches shorter at bottom, and you will have half the lining pattern (Fig. 127).

Make notches at one side of lining pattern and you will have indicated the center seams (Fig. 128a).

Fold it in half (Fig. 128b), and draw a heavy line on the crease to indicate the straight of grain proper for this lining (Fig. 128c). Easy, isn't it?

Fig. 128   Short gore skirt cutting guide

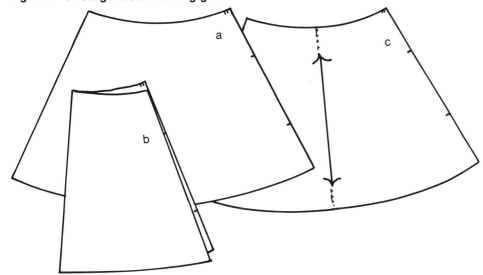

Cutting guide

For both skirts, cut through both fabrics for gores. Cut through one fabric only for belt.

Short skirt (across grain): Fig. 129a
Long skirt (across grain): Fig. 129b

Fig. 129   Long gore skirt cutting guide

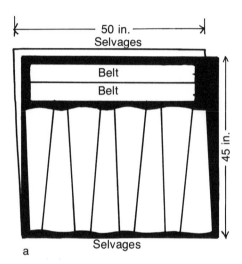

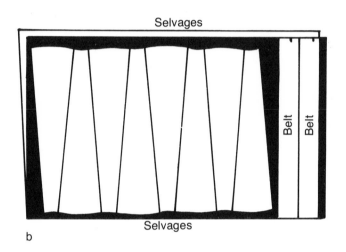

Fig. 130

How to sew

Decide first on the order in which you want the gores. Then, with right sides together, sew gore 1 to gore 2 (Fig. 130).

Next, sew gore 3 to 2, 4 to 3, etc., up to 8. Put the resulting piece aside.

Repeat, starting at gore 9, sewing 10 to 9, etc., up to 16.

Sew the two pieces of eight gores together (Fig. 131).

Sew under side edges (Fig. 132) if you aren't lining the skirt. Turn up hem.

Sew on belt, using any technique described in the book (for self belt, see Figs. 72–79).

For a lined skirt: Complete skirt body, press, and put aside. Sew the two pieces of lining fabric together at center seam, and turn up a narrow hem at the bottom.

With right side of lining to right side of skirt body, sew a $\frac{1}{2}$-inch seam down edges of backs (Fig. 133).

Turn to right sides, stitch along the top, matching center seams.

Stitch bottom edges and hem as in Figs. 109–110.

Sew belt (see Figs. 72–79 for self belt).

Press and wear!

Fig. 131

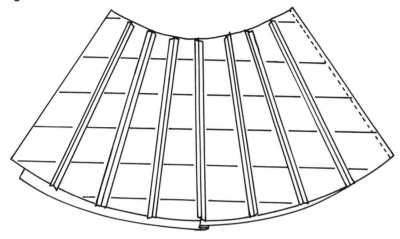

Fig. 132

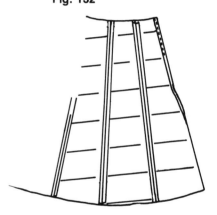

Fig. 133

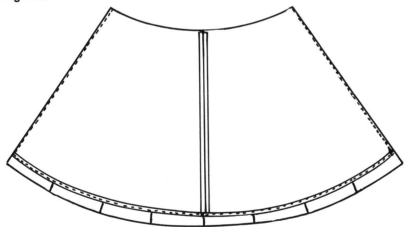

GORE SKIRT WITH DRAWSTRING OR ELASTICIZED WAIST

Materials needed for short and long skirt

The same as in the wrap skirt for sizes 12 to 16. For larger sizes, add as many gores as you need: each one gives you an extra $2\frac{1}{2}$ inches at the waist. Measure 7 inches down from the waist for the hip measurement, just to be sure you are adding enough pieces. If you are a size 10 or under, use fewer gores, unless your fabric is a very lightweight one that would look good in an almost dirndl effect. I find sixteen gores right for me. It gives an extra overlap I enjoy. I'm size 9 on my good days, a 10 on the bad.

Cutting guide (Figs. 128–129)

Eliminate belt, and instead cut a strip $1\frac{1}{2} \times 60$ inches to use for the tie for the drawstring skirt.

Cut a facing for the elasticized skirt. After sewing half the gores together, press and trace upper outline (Fig. 134).

Measure down $1\frac{1}{2}$ inches. Make notches for center top and center of facing (Fig. 135a). Cut out facing, fold it in half, and trim to make even, in case it isn't (Fig. 135b).

Cut two pieces of facing, using one for the front, one for the back, and use the fold to indicate straight of goods (Fig. 135c).

Fig. 134

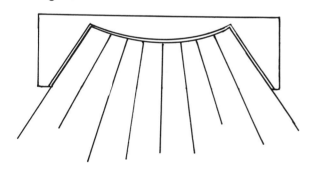

Fig. 135

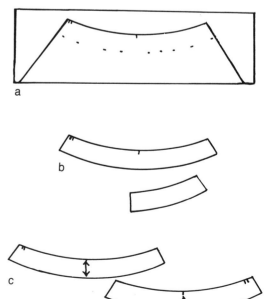

How to sew elasticized-waist gore skirt

Join gores, remembering to make facings at halfway mark.

Join all together, closing skirt. (Remember to sew from top to bottom.)

Prepare elastic as in Chapter 1 (see Fig. 19).

Sew facings together at side seams, using $\frac{1}{2}$-inch seams. Turn under $\frac{1}{4}$ inch on bottom of facing, with wrong sides together, and hold seams open as you sew over them (Fig. 136).

With right side of facing to right side of skirt, sew a $\frac{1}{2}$-inch seam along the top, making centers and sides meet (Fig. 137).

Turn facing to inside, and stitch at the edge of the right side of the skirt (about one-half the width of the presser foot) to hold the facing in place and to prevent the elastic from rolling up (Fig. 138).

With skirt side out (as in Fig. 139), insert elastic, sew along narrow hemstitch line, until there is no more elastic to sew. Then insert needle into fabric and pull the elastic toward you, moving gathers along and away. Even gathers, and continue stitching. You might have to do this several times before you insert all of the elastic.

As I said in Chapter 2, this is easier than it sounds, and will become logical to you as you sew. Check instructions and Figs. 54–55.

Make hem. Press and wear!

Fig. 136

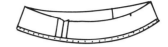

Fig. 137

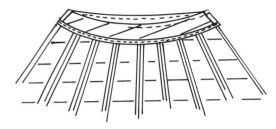

Fig. 138

Fig. 139

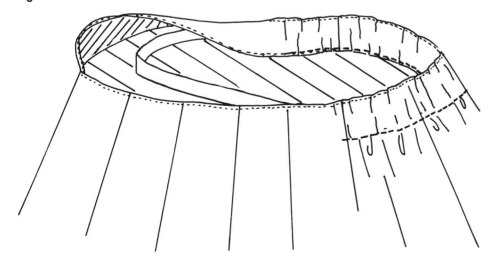

How to sew drawstring gore skirt

Sew one half the gores and make a facing (see Figs. 134–135).

Join all gores together.

Make two ⅝-inch buttonholes at either side of center seam of skirt (Fig. 140).

Prepare facings as in Fig. 136.

With right side of facing to right side of skirt, stitch a ½-inch seam at top, making centers and sides meet (see Fig. 137).

Turn facing to inside, and stitch right along the edge of the skirt (see Fig. 138). Sew tie (Fig. 141).

Work this section as in Fig. 142, with skirt side out, from the inside of the skirt. Put one end of tie through buttonhole closest to you, from inside out.

Stitch—thus making casing—starting 2 inches from the buttonhole. (Make sure not to stitch over tie.) Continue making sure that both facing seams and gore seams are open, until you come to the second buttonhole. Place tie through it, from inside of skirt out, and stitch to beginning stitch and backtack (Fig. 143).

Make knots on ends of ties so they won't slip out (Fig. 144).

Make hem.

Press and wear!

If you want to line either of the above skirts, make lining as described in wrap gore skirt (pages 66–67), sew both side seams together (the center becoming a side seam), and, with wrong side of lining to wrong side of skirt, sew along top using a ¼-inch seam to hold in place. Proceed as if there were no lining . . . but make sure the centers of fronts, backs, and side seams meet and match.

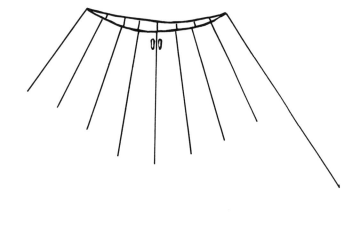

Fig. 140

Fig. 141

Fig. 142

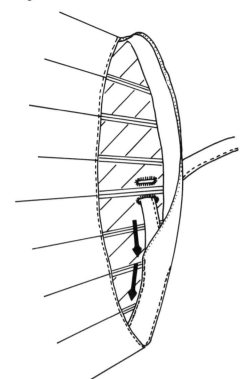

Fig. 143

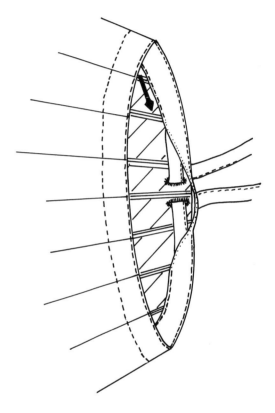

Fig. 144

Variations

If you make any of these, be sure to allow for the ½-inch seam at both the bottom of no. 1 and the top of no. 2 (fig. 145a).

You can make these skirts in solids with prints, different size prints, solids of different colors, colors of different tones outlined in ribbon—the possibilities are endless (see Figs. 145a–145c for some ideas).

Fig. 145

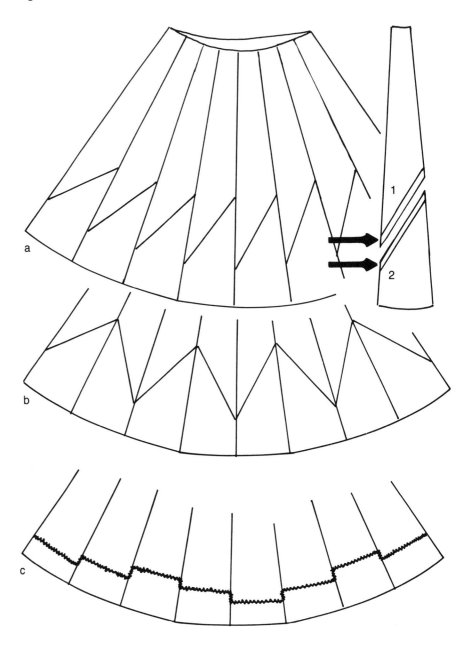

GORE SKIRT WITH POINTS (TIE EFFECT)
(Fig. 146)

Fig. 147

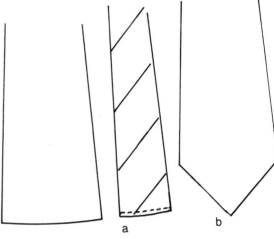

Materials and cutting guide

Same as for basic short or long gore skirt.

Fig. 146

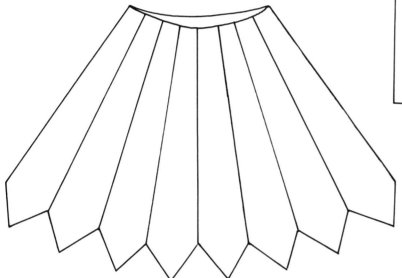

Fig. 148

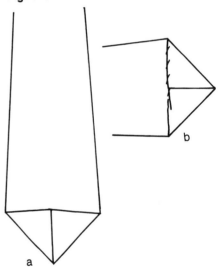

How to sew

Fold over each gore at the bottom, so that right sides are together, and stitch a $\frac{1}{2}$-inch seam across bottom (Fig. 147a). Turn to the right side. It will look like this (Fig. 147b) on the right side.

It will look like this (Fig. 148a) on the wrong side. Turn under the raw seam on back of pointed gore and slipstitch, or use any other kind of finishing stitch you choose (Fig. 148b).

Then, proceed as for the basic gore skirt, sewing from top to bottom (Fig. 149). Be sure to backtack at bottom, adjusting if need be so that the point effect will be even. This is a simple skirt—don't get to thinking it is difficult. Just be sure to do all the bottoms first . . . Make this up as a wrap, drawstring, or elasticized-waist skirt.

Press and wear!

Fig. 149

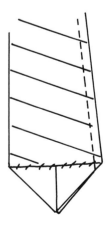

CHAPTER SIX

THE A-LINE DRAWSTRING SKIRT

The graceful shape of this skirt lends itself especially well to soft fabrics such as lightweight woolens. But, I've also made it in challis and cottons and crepes. Earlier this year I did a collection of summer clothes for a department store, and this skirt, in assorted soft cottons and rayon challis, was the runaway best seller!

Another advantage of this skirt is the ability of the waistline to expand with necessity. Or, another way of putting it is that, when you gain weight, you can just open up the tie a little more, and . . . instant comfort.

Fig. 150

BASIC DRAWSTRING SKIRT (Fig. 150)

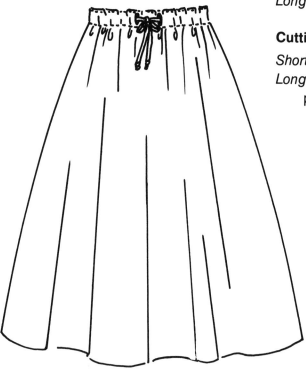

Materials needed

Short skirt: 1½ yards of 45-inch goods with grain
Long skirt: 2¼ yards of 45-inch goods

Cutting guide

Short skirt: Fig. 151
Long skirt: same layout as short skirt, with the addition of one piece 1½ × 18 inches and one piece 1½ × 45 inches

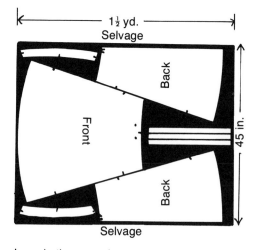

Fig. 151 Short drawstring skirt cutting guide

Long is the same layout.

How to sew

Make buttonholes on front of skirt. Starting at holes, work down for approximately ⅝ inch (see Fig. 140).

Join the 1½-inch strips, and, turning under edges, make a tie for the skirt (see Fig. 141).

Sew back pieces of skirt together, aligning notches (Fig. 152).

Sew front to back, aligning notches, working, as always, from top to bottom (Fig. 153).

Join facings at side seams. Turn under ¼ inch on bottom of facing, with wrong sides together.

Fig. 152

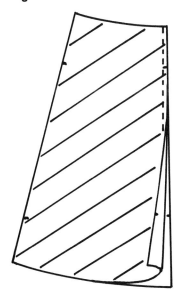

Fig. 153

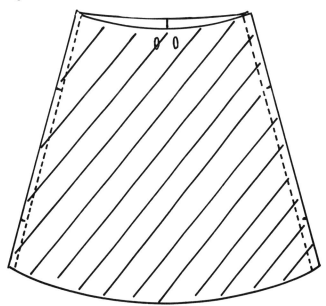

With right side of facing to right side of skirt, stitch at top using a $\frac{1}{4}$-inch seam—making sure seams are open and matching notches, etc. (see Fig. 137).

Turn facing to wrong side of skirt, and stitch along edge. You can use a $\frac{1}{8}$-inch or a $\frac{1}{4}$-inch seam allowance, take your choice . . . but you must do this in order to hold the tie in place, so that the top doesn't roll (see Fig. 138).

Keep outside of skirt (right side) out! Follow instructions and illustrations, Figs. 142–144.

Turn hem.

Press and wear!

RUFFLED TOP, RUFFLED BOTTOM (Fig. 154)

Materials needed

Short skirt: 1⅔ yards of 45-inch goods with grain.

The finished length of this skirt is 29 inches. Cut body 11 inches shorter than enclosed pattern. (If you want another length, or different proportions, I suggest you first make a marker.)

Long skirt: Use the same layout as for short skirt (Fig. 155), but use whole pattern pieces (the yardage will be 2½ yards of 45-inch goods with grain).

Cutting guide (Fig. 155)

Fig. 154

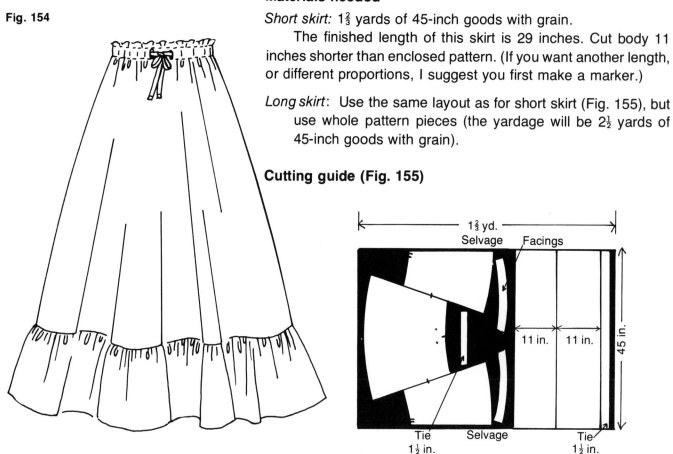

Fig. 155   Ruffled drawstring cutting guide (short skirt)

How to sew

Prepare facings (see Fig. 136).

Make buttonholes on front of skirt. Starting at hole, work down ⅝ inch (see Fig. 140).

Join the 18-inch piece to the 45-inch piece, and turn under raw edges for the tie (see Fig. 141).

Sew center back seam of skirt (see Fig. 152).

Join back to front of skirt (see Fig. 153).

With right side of facing to right side of skirt, join at top, aligning notches and seams, using a ¼-inch seam allowance.

Turn facing to inside of skirt, and, starting at back center seam, stitch ½ inch from the edge (Fig. 156). This extra width at edge provides the ruffle effect.

Insert tie through buttonhole, and follow instructions previously given for making a casing (Figs. 142–144).

Join the strips of ruffles—two pieces for the short skirt, three for the long.

Make a narrow hem on the bottom. (If your sewing machine has a hemming attachment leave one side open and do the narrow hem first, then close up that last seam.)

Make gathers at top of ruffle.

With right side of ruffle to right side of skirt bottom, adjust gathers, pin, and stitch with a ½-inch seam. Make sure that seams are open.

If you want to "finish" this seam, now is the time to pink lightly along the edge.

Turn seams up toward body of skirt, and, on the outside, stitch along bottom of skirt (Fig. 157a). The inside will look like this (Fig. 157b). This way the ruffle is held in place, and it will hang better. You can use any seam width you want, from $\frac{1}{16}$ inch to $\frac{3}{8}$ inch . . . it's a matter of aesthetics. Actually, the stitching won't show that much, so I do what is easiest for me . . . the width of the presser foot ($\frac{1}{4}$ inch).

Press and wear.

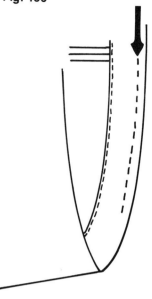

Fig. 156

Fig. 157

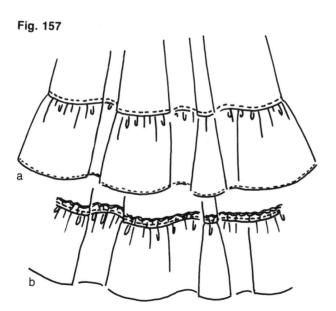

Comments

You don't have to make the ruffled top with the ruffled bottom—there is no reason you can't have one without the other. Also, if you want an even more exaggerated ruffle on top, say, of about 1 inch, just drop the buttonhole that much lower. But first, add that extra bit to the bottom of the facing when you cut, to compensate.

PATCHWORK RUFFLE DRAWSTRING SKIRT (Fig. 158)

I made this in cottons when I had small pieces of fabric that were too lovely to throw out. I just joined the assorted fabrics (all the same weight), and then made the ruffles out of them. The body of the skirt is a pale green print, almost a calico. The ruffle is made out of calicos in pinks. I put a binding of the pale green on the bottom of the ruffle. It was a great success. (I wore it with a pink tank top.)

Fig. 158

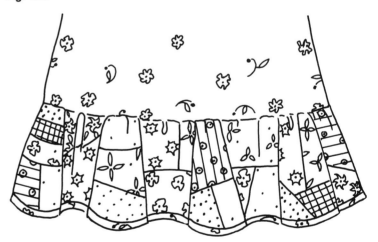

TIERED DRAWSTRING SKIRT (Fig. 159)

Materials needed

1 length of $1\frac{1}{2}$ yards of 45-inch goods
1 length of $2\frac{1}{4}$ yards of 45-inch goods

Cutting guide

See Fig. 151. Use *both* short and long, but cut only one tie and one set of facings.

How to sew

Prepare facings, following instructions in Fig. 136. Sew $\frac{1}{2}$-inch seam at sides.

Join the skirts, backs to front (Fig. 160).

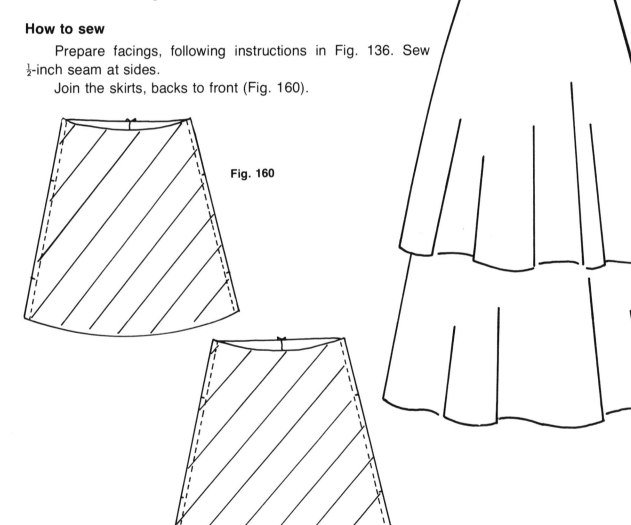

Fig. 159

Fig. 160

Prepare the tie, etc., but do not make the buttonholes!

Place the long skirt inside the short, and, aligning center back seams, notches, and side seams, right side out, sew together at the top edge.

Now make buttonholes, through *both* skirts (see Fig. 140 for buttonhole placement). Pin skirts flat around buttonhole area (Fig. 161).

Complete skirt as in Figs. 137–138, 142–144.

Press and wear!

Fig. 161

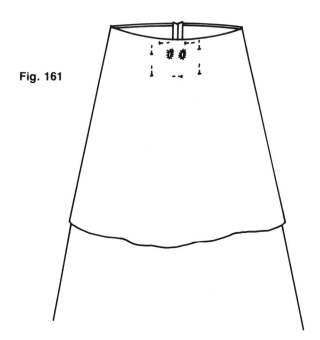

Comments

The preceding is for an evening-length skirt. If you want this tiered effect for daytime wear (I have made it in solid rust challis), cut two short skirts, and lop off the top one about 8 inches on the bottom. Please make a marker first, so you can save fabric! *Or* do it by eye, and waste fabric . . . trying it on and pinning the top one to get the proportion that suits you best.

This skirt can also be made with an elasticized waist.

This season the tiered skirt is very much in fashion—although I've always worn it, and always consider it in style. To supply myself with a variety of skirts by making only one new one, I took an old petticoat and sewed a very full ruffle in gray print chiffon to the bottom of it, and so far I've worn it under a gray wool skirt (elasticized rectangle), my solid rust challis, and a brown tweed gore wrap. Fig. 162 shows it under my daytime-length tiered challis.

Fig. 162

CHAPTER SEVEN

THE DENIM SKIRT

I think the denim skirt is American genius at work. Whoever thought it up gets my applause and thanks. It has saved me the pain of throwing away old jeans that were still good. It has also gotten my young daughter into a skirt—something she used to wear only for party occasions.

While writing this book, I wanted to experiment with a denim skirt for my editor. I went to her house and helped her pick out the pair of jeans she would "sacrifice." I was in luck, because they were straight legged. Not that you can't make a skirt from flare-legged jeans, but, the straighter the leg, the simpler the operation.

We decided on an evening look for them. I had scraps of satin, 7-inch squares, left over from the days at the factory. I parted with a lot when I gave up the business, but not those satin squares. I also have, and this is a little more unusual, several gross of satin buttons. I mean, you never know when you'll need a hundred or so of black, white, magenta, or turquoise satin buttons! Since she had just bought a new black silk blouse, I decided to use the black and white satin squares, and some of the black and white satin buttons along the bottom.

Fig. 163

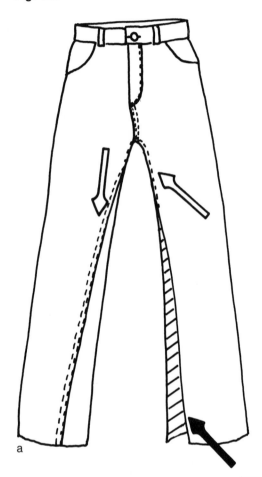

THE DENIM SKIRT WITH INSET (LONG AND SHORT)

Materials needed

One pair of jeans that fit you in the waist
1 yard of fabric
    or
denim scraps
    or
any scraps you have around the house
A couple of large sheets of newspaper

How to sew

Decide what length skirt you want, and, cutting carefully, cut jeans 3 inches longer than you want the finished skirt. (This is protection, to insure your getting a good curve later on.) If you want a long skirt, there is no need to cut at this time.

Rip carefully along inner seam on both legs (Fig. 163a).

Rip seams up front to almost the bottom of fly (Fig. 163b).

Rip back almost three-quarters of the way up (Fig. 163c).

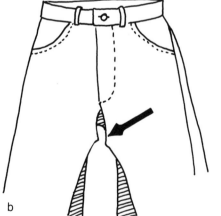

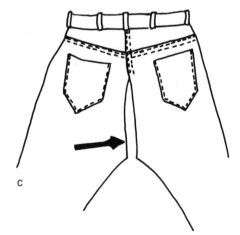

Fig. 164

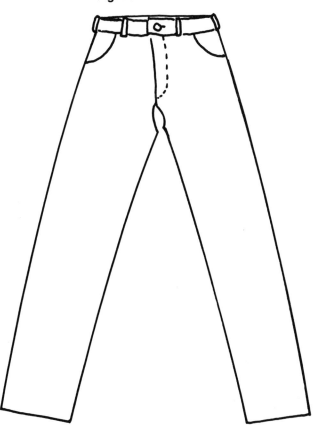

Fig. 165

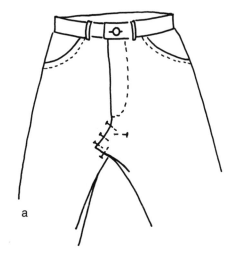

a

Put the pants on the floor, and spread the legs as far apart as you can, without making terrific creases and folds in the upper section (Fig. 164).

Pin the front sections in place, with left side over right, turning under seam allowance (Fig. 165a).

Repeat on back (Fig. 165b).

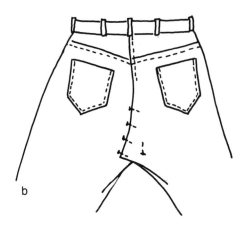

b

Take a large piece of paper, and, putting it under the front section, make a pattern of the triangular space. Draw a hemline, curving it. Do the same for the back. The front and back sections are sometimes quite different. Add two inches on each side and top for underlap and insurance. You can always cut away the extra. Also, mark the patterns front and back as soon as you make them, so you won't get them confused (Fig. 166).

Cut on solid lines.

Cut out fabric the shape of the front and back patterns.

Fig. 166

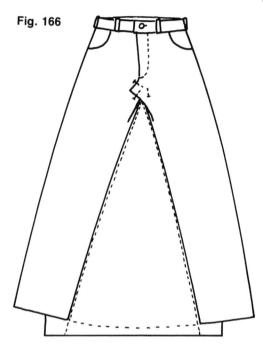

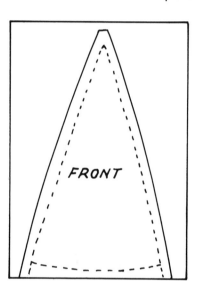

FRONT

Fig. 167

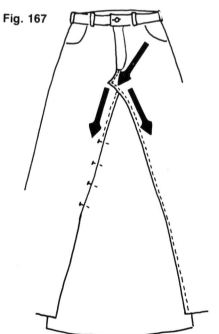

Fig. 168

Pin the jeans on top of the fabric.

Turn under the raw seams of the jeans (Fig. 167), and, backtacking first, sew from top to bottom from under the fly, along that curve, and down the leg. Then backtack again, and stitch down the other side. Repeat this step on the back.

Once more, place what is now a skirt on the flat cutting surface. Starting from the side-waist, and, going across skirt, mark skirt length with chalk—every couple of inches from top of back waist. Be sure to have side seams at the side, or in balance. For instance, some jeans skirts have a bit of the back toward the front (Fig. 168).

Also, please notice that the back is higher than the front in the illustration. This is the way jeans, and most pants, are made. So, when marking for the hem, have the pants front side up, but mark from the top of back waist. This way, the completed skirt will hang naturally.

Overcast bottom for hem, or turn it up and sew.

Press and wear!

Variations

Fig. 169a. Floral appliqué—cutting out print and applying to fabric.

Fig. 169b. Striped denim.

Fig. 169c. Rickrack contrast.

Fig. 169d. Button scallops.

Fig. 169e. Button triangles.

Fig. 169

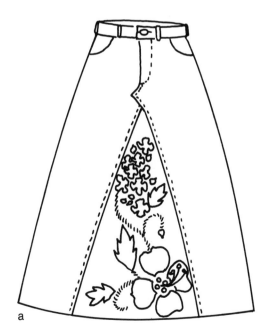

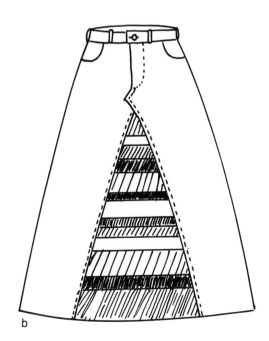

a   b

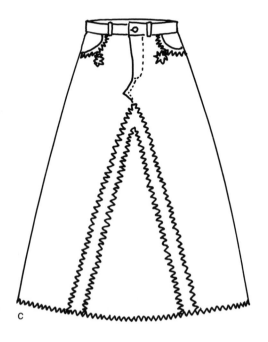

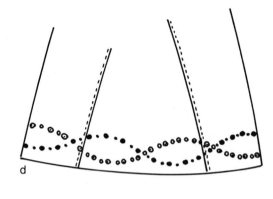

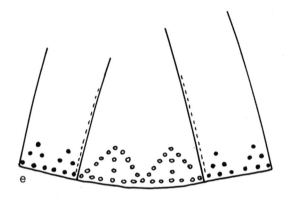

GATHERED DIRNDL JEAN SKIRT (Fig. 170)

Materials needed

1 pair of jeans that fit you in the waist and hips.

Assorted soft fabrics (crepes, challis, lightweight cottons, etc.):
  a single piece that is 21 × 54 inches and assorted much
  smaller pieces with which to make ruffles (see Fig. 170).
  There is no rule to determine how many rows of ruffles to
  apply. That is up to you. *But*, the minimum size rectangle
  is 21 × 54 inches for the base. Anything smaller won't give
  you enough leg room, and will look clumsy.

Assorted ribbon.

Fig. 170

Fig. 171

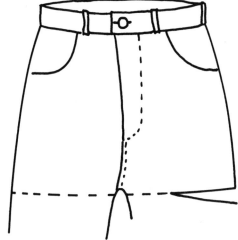

How to sew

Holding the jeans properly, so that the back is higher than the front (Fig. 171), measure about 12 inches from the top of the waist down, and cut.

Cut (rip) open inner seams, and rip seams up front to fly, and up the back (see Figs. 163a, 163b, 163c).

Do not spread out as in basic jeans skirt!

Pin closed, following the natural shape of the jeans.

Stitch front and back closed (Fig. 172).

Fig. 172

Fig. 173

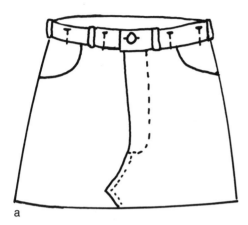

a

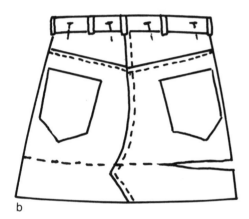

b

Now, centering jeans, so that they fall naturally and the back is higher than the front, pin closed at waist (Fig. 173a).

Turn over so that back is up, and measure from the top of the waist down to the bottom of the pocket. Add 1 inch, and mark with tailor's chalk across the jeans, and cut (Fig. 173b).

Cut two small strips, from the small pieces of soft fabric you've put aside—1½ × 10 inches each. Turn under all four sides of strips with narrow hem on both pieces. Measure the edge of the front pockets, and gather these strips to a little less than that measurement. Sew along edge of pockets—this is tedious, but worth the effort, since it really gives the skirt a unique look (Fig. 174).

Make hem on large rectangle.

Cut assorted pieces of fabric to measure 90 × 4 inches, with which to make ruffles. The minimum length is 90 inches. You can obtain these by cutting across 45-inch goods twice, and then joining the two resulting strips.

Turn under hem, make gathers, and apply to rectangle, with right side of ruffle to right side of fabric, and with ruffle "up" (Fig. 175). Sew down ruffle at side edges.

Use as many or as few ruffles as you like.

Apply ribbon.

Sew rectangle together, matching tops of ruffles, ribbon, etc.

Gather rectangle.

Fig. 174

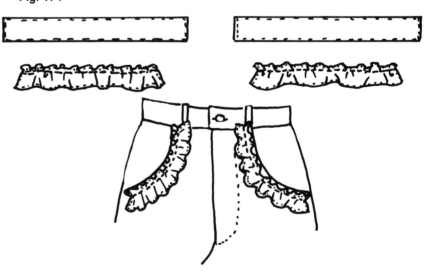

Fig. 175

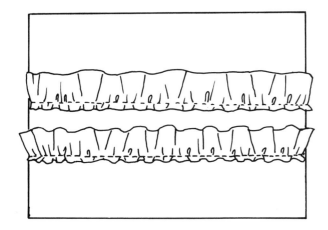

With the right side of fabric to the right side of jeans, stitch (making sure the gathers are even) with a $\frac{1}{2}$-inch seam. To prevent breaking the needle, sew slowly over the thickest parts of the jeans.

Topstitch from outside, with seam toward jeans, right along edge (Fig. 176).

Trim seams if you haven't cut out fabric with pinking shears. Press and wear!

Fig. 176

Variations

Fig. 177a. Denim patches.
Fig. 177b. Men's ties.
Fig. 177c. Vertical ruffle.

Fig. 177

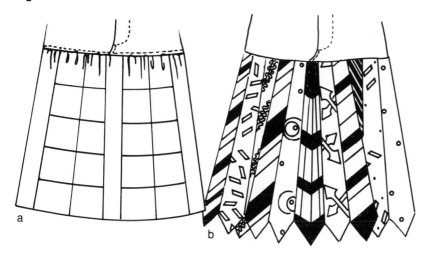

LATTICEWORK SKIRT (Fig. 178)

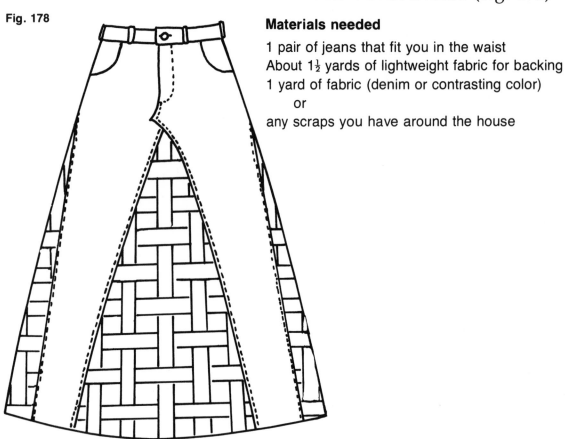

Fig. 178

Materials needed

1 pair of jeans that fit you in the waist
About 1½ yards of lightweight fabric for backing
1 yard of fabric (denim or contrasting color)
        or
any scraps you have around the house

How to sew

Prepare skirt as in Denim Skirt with Inset (see Figs. 163–166).
Rip open the side seams, to about where the hips end.

Follow instructions you used for the front insets for these side ones as well . . . making a paper pattern.

Cut out the four pattern pieces (the front, back, and two sides) in the lightweight fabric . . . marking them ("front," "back," "right side," "left side") so that you won't lose track of which is which.

Cut fabric in which you want to do the latticework (with the grain of fabric) in 3-inch-wide strips.

Sew strips with ¼-inch seam, being careful to keep edges aligned and right sides together (Fig. 179).

Turn and press, so that the seam is not on the edge, but so that it is in the middle of the strip (Fig. 180).

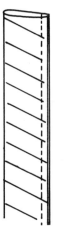

Fig. 179   Fig. 180

Measuring from top of inset, mark in pencil 2 inches down on the right side, and mark down that side every 3 inches (Fig. 181). From the left side start at 2 inches down, and *then* mark every 3 inches.

Working from the bottom up, pin strips at edges from right to left, last mark to last mark, etc. (Fig. 182). Cut. Don't use a new strip until you have used up every bit of the last one.

Starting at the center top, weave down, over one strip, under the next, until you reach the bottom edge. Pin edges (Fig. 183).

Measure 3 inches from the center of that strip on right and left, and weave strips. Pin at edges (Fig. 184).

When the inset is complete, sew along edges, remove pins. Pin prepared jeans to top of finished latticework and complete garment as for Denim Skirt with Inset (see Figs. 167–168). The only difference is that this skirt will also have side insets.

Press, wear, and get compliments!

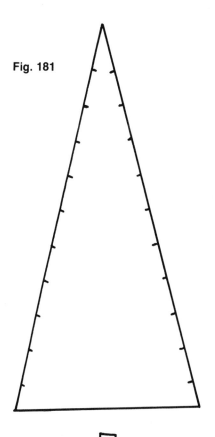

Fig. 181

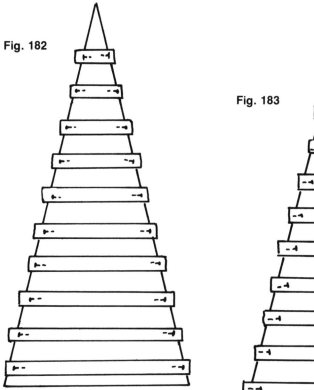

Fig. 182

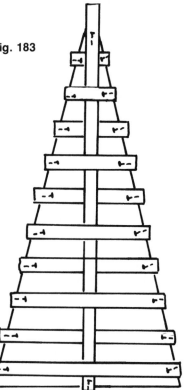

Fig. 183

Fig. 184

CHAPTER EIGHT

THE CIRCLE

This is the first skirt I can remember making. Before I knew anything about patterns, even about the *idea* of a right and a wrong way to sew, I remember cutting and sewing a circle skirt. My mother, who was a dress designer, and who taught me to sew, was always scandalized at my approach to this skirt. But then, the way I cut it, and the way I sewed it, was the way all my friends in Brooklyn did in the nineteen thirties and forties.

Although I never manufactured this skirt, I think enough of it to adapt it for you. It's as though I've rediscovered an old friend who's improved with age.

The main improvement is in the finishing. We used to leave one seam open at the top, and, applying a belt and using a series of hooks and eyes, the skirt was closed by overlapping. It doesn't sound as bad as it looked. But we were young then, and, I suppose, our youth supplied a kind of beauty that made everything we wore wonderful.

HOW TO MAKE A PATTERN FOR YOUR CIRCLE SKIRT

Mark one edge of a 36-inch-square piece of paper "seam line" and mark the other "center fold."

Mark corners "A," "B," and "C."

Make notches in two places along seam lines: at 15 inches and at 25 inches (Fig. 185).

Fold corner C over to meet corner B. Crease sharply—please try to be exact (Fig. 186).

Fold over BC to creased edge (the arrow is pointing to it), and mark "D" on the corner you've just made (Fig. 187).

Now measure 5½ inches from A to D, from A to BC, and a few times in between. This will indicate the waistline (Fig. 188).

Cut along these lines.

Measure from this edge toward D and BC, and in between, and mark for skirt hem (Fig. 189). I measure 30 inches; if you want a shorter skirt, measure less. Cut out pattern.

For a longer length, you will have to start with a larger square of paper.

Fig. 185

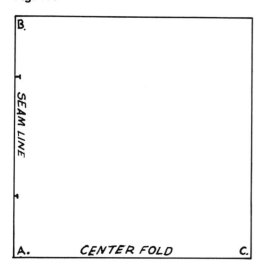

Fig. 186

Fig. 187

Fig. 188

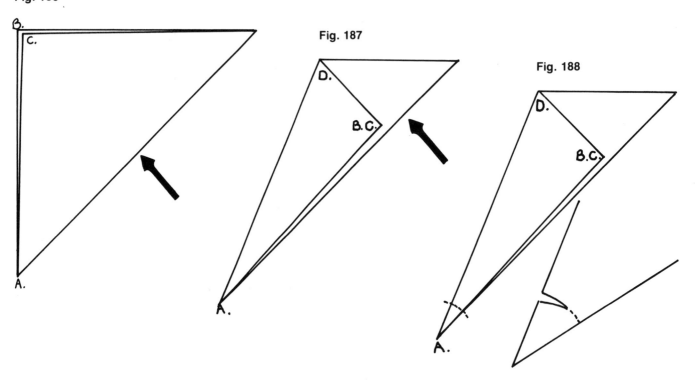

Fig. 189

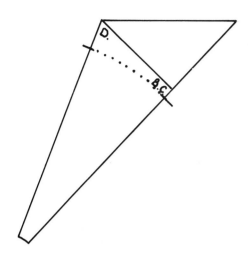

Fig. 190

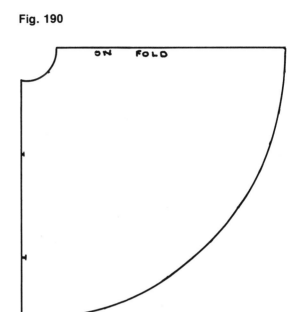

Fig. 191

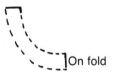

Your pattern should look like Fig. 190 when opened. Make a notch in the center of waistline and above one edge. Mark other edge "on fold."

To make a facing, trace outline of top edge, and down 2 inches on sides. Mark one edge "on fold," and put a notch in the other edge (Fig. 191).

You now have a pattern for the circle skirt. Congratulations!

This skirt will fit over 39-inch hips. If your hips are larger than this, cut pattern waistline at 6 inches below point A (instead of $5\frac{1}{2}$ inches), and you'll be surprised by how much room you'll gain.

CIRCLE SKIRT AS A WRAP (Fig. 192)

Fig. 192

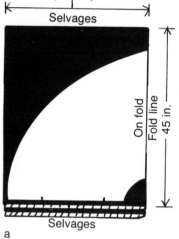

Material needed

4 yards of 45-inch goods *without* nap

Cutting guide (Figs. 193a, 193b, 193c)

Fig. 193   Circle wrap cutting guide

4 yd. folded into 1 yd. Be sure to have the two fold lines exactly on top of each other.

Selvages

On fold
Fold line
45 in.

Selvages

a

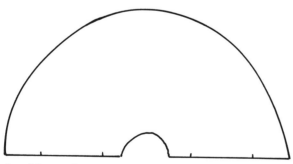

b   After cutting you will have two pieces that look like this.

c   Cut belt from piece left over. Cut in one continuous piece.

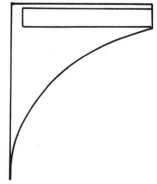

How to sew

Prepare belt by cutting a piece of fabric 4 × 90 inches from piece left over after you have cut the skirt.

Make notches in center on both sides, and then make notches 17 inches from that on either side. This will mark the center band, and the piece will be 34 inches long (Fig. 194).

With right sides of belt together, sew from notch to end and across on both ends (Fig. 195). Turn, and recut all the notches *except* the center one, so that they are a full $\frac{1}{2}$ inch.

With the right sides together, sew down the two pieces of skirt along one side, using a $\frac{1}{2}$-inch seam. Align notches, as usual. Turn under a narrow hem on the two remaining edges, ignoring the notches on these (Fig. 196).

Fig. 194

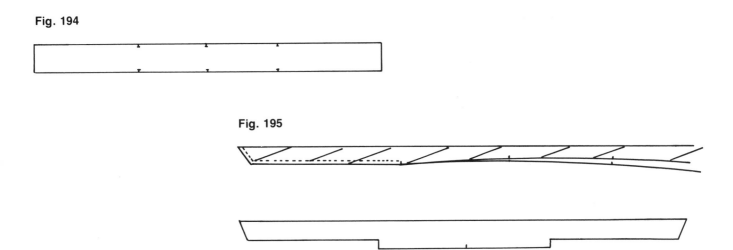

Fig. 195

Fig. 196

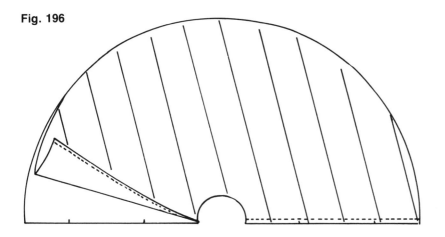

Fig. 197

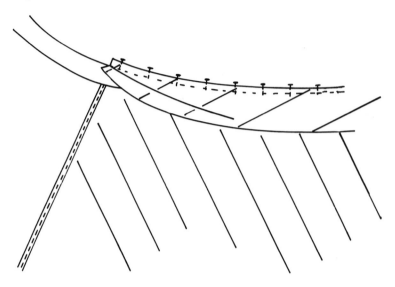

With right side of belt to wrong side of skirt, the edge of the skirt to the notch, skirt side up, sew a ½-inch seam (Fig. 197). (Only sew one edge of the belt. The other side is for the front.)

Fold over a ½-inch seam allowance on the remaining edge of the belt (Fig. 198a), and topstitch over previous stitching line (Fig. 198b). (Review belt in Figs. 72–79.)

Hang up skirt for twenty-four hours or so. This is most important! The skirt will dip and be uneven, the weight of the fabric pulling it down, especially the parts that hang on the bias. So, to save yourself trouble, hang it up, and let it "do its thing." Only after it has hung for at least a day should you put it on, mark the hem, cut it evenly, and hem it.

Press and wear!

Fig. 198

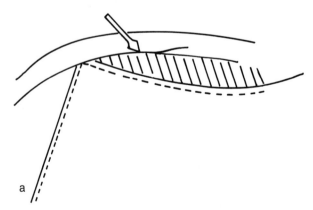

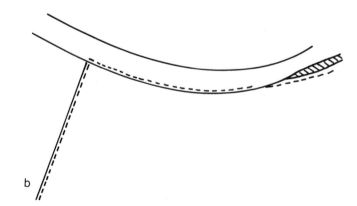

a

b

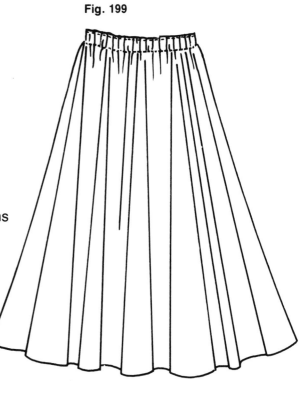

Fig. 199

ELASTICIZED CIRCLE SKIRT (Fig. 199)

Materials needed

4 yards of fabric, 45 inches wide
1 yard of elastic

Cutting guide

Cut the same as Fig. 193. Do not cut belt, but cut two facing pieces from leftover fabric (Fig. 200). See directions for facing, Fig. 191.

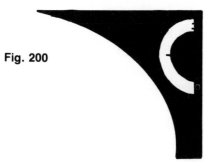

Fig. 200

How to sew

Prepare elastic as in Chapter 1, Fig. 19.

With right sides together, join facings, aligning notches. Use a $\frac{1}{2}$-inch seam.

Turn under $\frac{1}{4}$ inch on bottom of facing, wrong side to wrong side.

With right sides together, join the two pieces of skirt. Align notches, and use a $\frac{1}{2}$-inch seam.

With right sides together, stitch the facing to the skirt, using a $\frac{1}{4}$-inch seam (width of your presser foot), matching seams and notches (Fig. 201).

Fig. 201

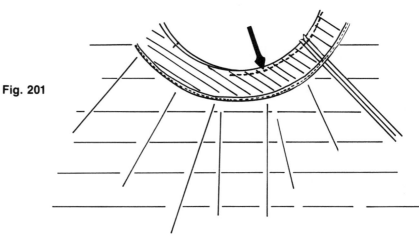

Fig. 202

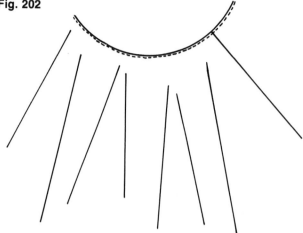

Turn facing to inside and topstitch on outside of skirt, right along the edge (Fig. 202).

Insert elastic, sewing along previously stitched bottom of facing (See Figs. 54–55).

Hang up skirt for at least twenty-four hours!

Put on skirt, and mark hem.

Hem.

Press and wear!

Fig. 203

THE POINT CIRCLE SKIRT (Fig. 203)

This skirt is for the adventurous, and wearing it takes a bit of courage. It is simple to make. I wear it for formal parties and around the holiday season. Since this skirt is so overpowering, wear a very simple top with it. My point skirt is in a burgundy lightweight wool, with a wide burgundy grosgrain ribbon at the bottom edges. I wear a simple high-necked blouse of the same fabric with the skirt, and a gold chain for jewelry. Nothing more than that. The skirt is enough.

Fig. 204

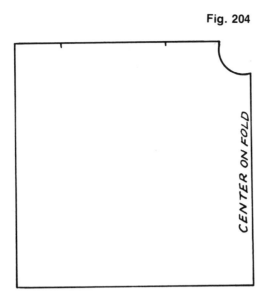

Pattern for Point Circle Skirt

Follow instructions that begin this chapter (see Figs. 185–188). Your pattern will look like Fig. 204. Make notches above one edge, and mark the other edge "center fold."

Make the facing as in Fig. 191.

Materials needed

4 yards of a soft, graceful fabric 45 inches wide
1 yard of elastic
$4\frac{1}{4}$ yards of a good ribbon, either grosgrain or satin—$1\frac{1}{2}$–3 inches wide.

Cutting guide (Fig. 205)

Cut facings from leftover fabric. For the belt, you can cut one continuous piece measuring 90 × 5 inches.

How to sew

Follow instructions for Elasticized Circle Skirt, but stop when you come to the part that tells you to hang up the skirt. You don't have to hang this skirt. Its very unevenness is part of its charm.

Fig. 205   Point circle skirt cutting guide

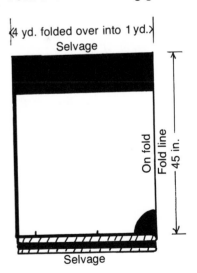

Fig. 206

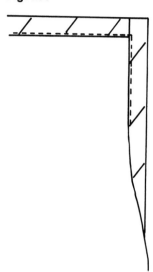

Turn a ½-inch edge to the right side along the whole of the bottom (Fig. 206).

Starting at one corner, sew ribbon over the narrow hem, with the edge of the ribbon right to the edge of the fabric (Fig. 207a). Either miter when you come to next corner, or fold over ribbon so that it is even with edges (Fig. 207b).

Stitch along top edge of ribbon. For the sake of appearance, do this stitching the same distance from the edge as the stitching along the bottom (Fig. 208).

Press and wear!

Fig. 207

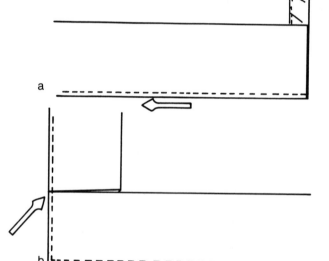

a

b

Fig. 208

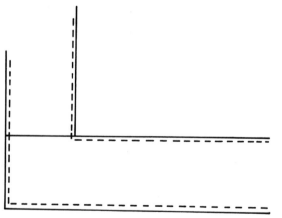

CHAPTER NINE

TRIMS AND . . .

This chapter is for you to have fun with. You need not use exactly the ideas I've drawn, but let these ideas help open up your own creative instincts.

For instance, I have shown how to make petals for an appliqué flower. I envision that flower on a denim skirt. There is no reason for you to limit yourself to a single flower. Why not petals falling loosely over the skirt hem? Or used as a single rose, with embroidered stem? Or as accent in a stitched bouquet of flowers you've cut from a printed fabric. . . .

I find "playing" with paper invaluable. I try out shapes by folding them in paper first, and I know nothing of the Japanese art of origami . . . I just press a little here, pinch a little there, testing out my ideas. There are rulers with scallops on them, but I've never used one. I'm a firm believer in folding the paper over several times, finding the right-size jar cover, and cutting. Very unprofessional, I know, but a habit from my days as a paper-doll fan.

Use the ideas in this section as shown, or make up others, but use trims, sashes, belts, and pockets to make your clothes even more your own.

209. The circular ruffle.

This ruffle takes a lot of fabric, but has a special feminine look, perhaps because of the delicate way the fabric falls.

Be sure to have all the grains of fabric going in the same direction when cutting, so that when you join pieces they will all fall in the same way.

The larger the inner circle the more flare. I suggest that you cut a variety of paper circles and experiment with different widths, etc., before you cut fabric. Refer to the drawing when you have decided what width and size circle you will cut, and be sure to join the pieces on the straight of the grain.

Fig. 209

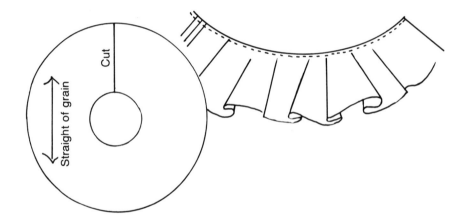

210a. Top-edge ruffle.

Ruffling of straight goods either on the straight of goods or across it, with the top edge a ruffle itself. Applied on the *outside* of the garment.

Fig. 210a

Fig. 210b

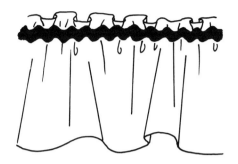

210b. Trimmed top-edge ruffle.

Trim over stitching. You can use rickrack, ribbon, floral trims, or even make a binding of a contrasting color.

211. Ruffle with binding trim.

Ruffling of straight goods either on the straight of goods or across it, with binding on edge of ruffle, top and bottom, and over the seam line. I did this for a mauve corduroy skirt, and used rust trim.

Fig. 211

Fig. 212

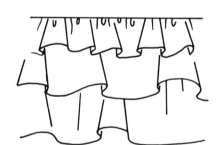

212. Tiered ruffles.

I think they speak for themselves. There is no reason you can't stitch fabrics together to make a patchwork for each ruffle. These, too, are straight of goods or across fabric.

213. Ruched ruffle.

Straight of goods or across grain ruffle, joined to the fabric by stitching in the center. This looks wonderful with a ribbon trim down the middle.

214. Scallops.

See Chapter 1, Fig. 16.

Fig. 213

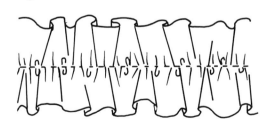

Fig. 214

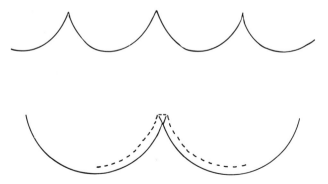

215. Points.

Clip into corners, trim points. A very useful decorative touch for just about everything.

Fig. 215

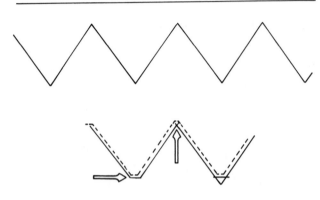

Fig. 216

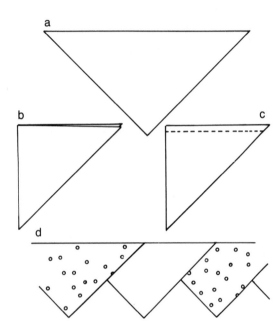

216. Triangles.

a) Separate triangles.
b) Fold over.
c) Sew across top.
d) Turn, and use for decorative trim.

217. Petals and leaves—some possible shapes.

Fig. 217

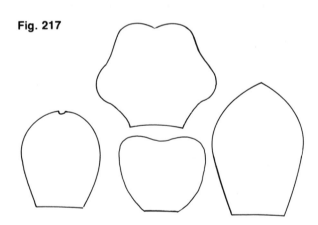

218. Pinched petals.

a) Sew petals close to edge of fabric, with wrong sides together.
b) Turn.
c) "Pinch" to give a natural look. Pin to keep this way until sewn onto garment.
d) Appliqué, using petals.

Fig. 218

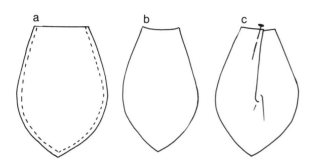

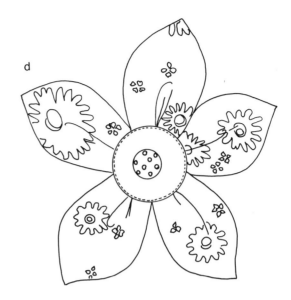

219. Tassels.

a) Wind yarn around a piece of cardboard approximately the length of the tassel you want. Slip a piece of yarn between yarn and cardboard when your tassel reaches the desired fullness— remember to consider the yarn on both sides of the cardboard.
b) Make a tight knot.
c) Cut bottom edge, releasing the yarn. Tie a second knot and trim the bottom even.

220. Pouch pocket.

a) Gather top of semicircle.
b) Apply binding, either contrast or self fabric. Cut out different size papers first, and pin these to fabric before you cut it.

Fig. 219

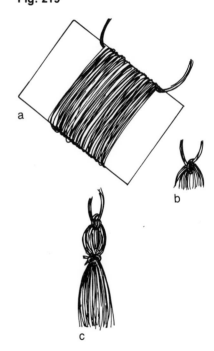

Fig. 220

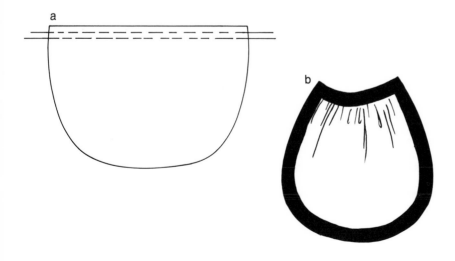

221. Patch pocket.

a) Turn under small amount on top of pocket, wrong sides together.

b) Turn this stitched edge to right side to create a facing—about 1½–2 inches. Stitch a ½-inch seam down sides. Trim corners.

c) Turn facing to wrong side, turn under ½-inch seam to wrong side. Either press or pin to keep in place.

d) Pin pocket in place on skirt. Stitch close to edge. Reinforce upper part of pocket so that it won't pull out with wear. You can make a triangle, a box, or just double stitch.

Fig. 221

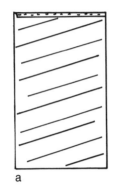

a

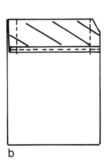

b

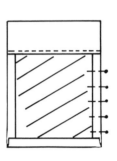

d

222. Use of some trims on pockets.

Fig. 222

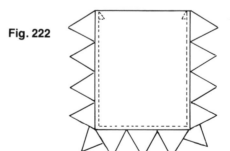

223. Belts and sashes.

224. Some end treatments for sashes and belts.

Fig. 223

Fig. 224

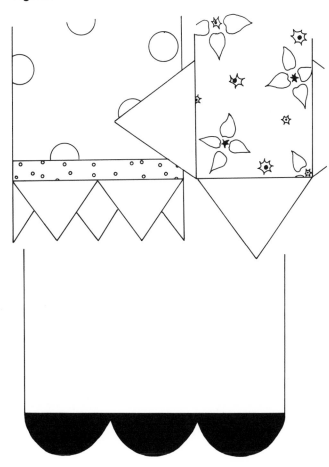

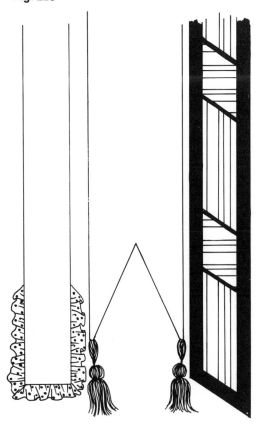

METRIC EQUIVALENTS TABLE

Metric to English
1 centimeter = .4 inch
1 meter = 3.3 feet
1 meter = 1.1 yards
1 square meter = 1.2 square yards

English to Metric
1 inch = 2.5 centimeters
1 foot = .3 meter
1 yard = .9 meter
1 square yard = .8 square
   meter

LINING SELECTION CHART

Skirt Fabric	Lining
sheer to lightweight cottons and blends	batiste; lawn; silklike polyester lining
silk; lace; lightweight crepe	china silk; silklike rayon or polyester lining; lightweight crepe
medium-weight wools, cottons, silks	lightweight taffeta; lawn, or any sheer cotton; china silk; silk surrah; silklike rayon
heavyweight cottons, wools; corduroy; tweed; brocades	polished cottons; lightweight cotton; medium-weight taffeta; crepe; satin